BACK TO ME

NEW DEGREE PRESS
COPYRIGHT © 2021 CHANDRA KENNETT
All rights reserved.

BACK TO ME
A Lifetime of Lessons Learned and Unlearned

ISBN
978-1-63730-667-3 *Paperback*
978-1-63730-756-4 *Kindle Ebook*
978-1-63730-870-7 *Digital Ebook*

BACK TO ME

A Lifetime of Lessons
Learned and Unlearned

CHANDRA KENNETT

To my SONshines, you both make me so happy, even when skies aren't gray. You've taught me everything I never knew about unconditional love and I feel so lucky to call you mine.

To everyone I've encountered on my journey: we met for a reason and I appreciate whatever lessons we taught each other.

CONTENTS

AUTHOR'S NOTE		11
PART 1.	**THE LEARNING**	**19**
CHAPTER 1		23
CRICKETS		24
EGGSHELLS		26
SANCTUARIES		31
MANNEQUINS		33
CHAPTER 2		37
BFFS		37
PHASES		40
PATTERNS		43
CHAPTER 3		47
ISLANDS		47
SCISSORS		51
TECHNIQUES		54
CHAPTER 4		59
LADDERS		59
PROPOSALS		64
BIRTHS		68
PART 2.	**THE RECALCULATING**	**73**
CHAPTER 5		75
INTRODUCTIONS		75
GOODBYES		79
TISSUES		83

CHAPTER 6	87
PRAYERS	87
DOSES	93
PATHS	96
CHAPTER 7	101
RENEWALS	101
BREAKDOWNS	104
FUMES	108
PART 3. THE UNLEARNING	**115**
CHAPTER 8	117
BEGINNINGS	117
ENDINGS	120
FIRES	124
CHAPTER 9	127
TRUTHS	127
MEETINGS	131
SIGNS	134
AWAKENINGS	138
CHAPTER 10	141
RETREATS	141
ZONES	144
PIVOTS	147
LESSONS	150
CHAPTER 11	155
HIKES	155
ACCIDENTS	157
FEATHERS	160
EPILOGUE	165
ACKNOWLEDGMENTS	169
APPENDIX	173

DISCLAIMER

The stories in this book are my memory of events as they happened. As a memoirist, I share my journey from my perspective. There are no villains in my story, only other humans on their own personal journeys. To protect their anonymity, I've changed all the names and shifted timelines slightly. I have also chosen to leave out some important people and events that definitely impacted my life in many ways but didn't directly affect this particular journey—the journey back to me.

One day you will tell your story of how you overcame what you went through and it will be someone else's survival guide.

—BRENÉ BROWN

AUTHOR'S NOTE

It was August 2016 when I found myself in the *in-between,* an uncertain place that resided halfway between a new life unknown to me and an old life where I had become unknown to myself. Divorce was on the table. I teetered on a precipice and needed to make a choice.

I could choose to stay with the man I'd spent the previous nine years with. I could stay because we took vows and I felt I owed it to both of us to make it work. I could, but we'd been working on our relationship for over a year and nothing had changed. I knew him and what I was getting—a handsome husband with a successful career. A provider. A life that looked great on paper. I also knew what I was *not* getting and likely never would. Things I needed to stay alive just as much as air or water: empathy, support, and respect.

I could choose to stay for my children, who at the time were only two and six. It would be so easy to sweep all our marital issues under the proverbial rug, just to be able to snuggle my babies to sleep each night. I always thought I would do anything for them. But, as it turned out, I couldn't do that. Staying in the life I'd come to resent and continuing the charade, even for their sake, was agonizing. I couldn't allow them to grow up thinking this was what a happy healthy relationship looked like. They deserved a chance for something better.

I could choose to turn back and run toward the familiar, but what good would that do? What had become familiar was the constant ache in my chest and the tears on my pillow each night. What had become familiar was waking up every morning and not recognizing the woman in the mirror.

Or I could choose to leave. To plunge forward into an abyss. A looming darkness calling out to me, terrifying me every bit as much as it thrilled me.

If I could go back to my thirty-nine-year-old self and comfort her, to tell her how everything would work out in the end, I don't know if I would. She needed to face the darkness and jump without knowing the outcome. She had to trust in herself. In her inner knowing. In the little voice that had begged her to leave for years. She had to have faith everything would work out the way it was supposed to.

It was around this time I began reading Glennon Doyle Melton's new-at-the-time book, *Love Warrior* (Melton, 2016). The memoir of a woman who spent much of her life hiding from her true self because the act of *feeling* hurt too much.

I had never felt more understood.

"Crisis means to sift. Let it all fall away and you'll be left with what matters," Melton wrote. "What matters most cannot be taken away."

I thought about this often while I was in the *in-between*. I thought about how my life was in the process of sifting, shifting back and forth. I wondered what I'd be left with at the end.

I look back on the summer of 2016 with so many different emotions. Sadness for feeling like I was ripping my little family apart. Fear that I was making a huge mistake. Courage for finally standing up for myself and setting boundaries. And hope that I was making the right decision.

Falling forward into the unknown would simultaneously be one of the scariest and most freeing experiences of my life. Even as my feet descended from the crumbling rocks of the life I had once known and my stomach dropped in a free fall, I knew I would be okay.

I could already feel myself growing wings.

I hope this book stays with you for a long time. I hope it rewards you with a feeling of recognition. Recognition of me as a fellow traveler on this journey of life. Recognition of all the ways we are the same and all the ways we are not, so we can learn from each other. Maybe you'll even recognize parts of yourself you've never examined or validated.

You see, I believe we are all born as our true selves. Pure and innocent—not questioning our worth or our place in this world. But then we become conditioned by our families, communities, teachers, and peers. We form belief systems based on those of our loved ones. We develop a specific lens through which to view the world. This lens is not noticed, much less questioned, until we're older and reach a crossroads in our lives. For many, this crossroads is referred to as a midlife "crisis."

But remember, "crisis" means "to sift."

It is during this midlife "crisis" when we begin to uncover and identify those beliefs we've carried all of our lives. It's an opportunity to shine a light on those ideas we've held onto for so long. A time to determine which are true and which are not. A new perspective becomes clear.

It is during this time of "crisis" when we are able to reframe the beliefs that do not serve who we truly are. We are able to reconnect with our authentic selves. I believe that's why we're here, on this earth. To learn and grow and evolve back into the person we were always meant to be.

This book has been writing itself for so long, I'm not even sure when I made the decision to put it on paper. It's been the running dialogue in my head and heart for as long as I can remember. Every time I encountered an obstacle in my life, a new chapter appeared.

Over the course of nearly four decades, I learned who the world wanted me to be. I learned if I was agreeable, then I was worthy of love. I learned if I was quiet, then I was worthy of attention. I learned if I folded myself inside out to make others less uncomfortable, then I was worthy—period.

Each lesson learned was a domino, lined up with precision. I spent my whole life learning how to be what the world wanted me to be, carefully positioning each black and white game piece according to other people's rules. The pride I felt in having them all perfectly placed fueled me forward, until one event changed the course of my life.

The precariousness of these little pieces of plastic became glaringly obvious. The precariousness of life itself.

It only takes one tap to knock them all down.

Clattering all the way back to the beginning, the dominos of my life toppled one by one. What felt at the time like crisis began to feel more like reawakening. As each domino fell, a limiting belief crashed to the ground. As each domino fell, the armor that had kept me safe, but hidden, began to crack. As each domino fell, I got closer and closer to the real me.

My midlife "crisis" taught me I am more than I had ever thought possible. I am worthy of everything I desire simply because I am *me*.

It also allowed me to see how our lives can be divided into three parts, each of which is a necessary step to becoming the people we're meant to be.

The first part—the learning phase—can last for decades. This is the beginning. Step by step, we follow the path unfolding ahead of us. As children, we learn who to be and how to act. As young adults, we learn what is expected of us and what we need to do to be accepted in the world. Learning and learning and learning, every single day.

And then, suddenly, a crossroads. The path we've been on for so long splits in two. If we try to continue down the old path, the robotic GPS voice of our life laments "recalculating" over and over in an exasperated tone. We're no longer on the right path. Things aren't adding up. Something feels off, and we can't explain it.

This second part—the recalculating phase—is the midlife "crisis." This is when we're forced to acknowledge the loud repeating voice of the GPS and backtrack to the fork in the road. This is an invitation to start clearing a new path, sweeping away debris and removing any branches and rocks blocking the way forward. This might take months, maybe years—the length of time doesn't matter. We just know when the second path is clear, it's time to follow it. This may seem scary at first, but somehow, deep in our soul, we know it's meant for us. And once we begin moving forward, the third part—the unlearning phase—begins.

The unlearning phase is where we spend the rest of our life. Unlearning all the information that held us back. Unlearning all of the lies. Unlearning all the beliefs standing in the way of us becoming our most authentic selves.

My learning phase lasted thirty-six years, my recalculating phase lasted three years, and I'm currently on year five of my unlearning phase. This book is divided into these three parts and is a culmination of all the key moments of my life. The good moments, yes, but also the hard moments, the scary moments, and the sad moments. And all of the lessons that finally made sense in retrospect.

I felt I was supposed to share them, not necessarily to keep people from making the same mistakes I made (mistakes are how we learn after all), but to help others feel less alone. To inspire and empower them to reconnect with their authentic self. To uncover their truth. To find their way back.

My story is one of waking up one morning and no longer recognizing myself. A story of childhood emotional abandonment which led to decades of people pleasing (self-abandonment) in adulthood. It's the story of my midlife "crisis" and the journey back to me.

It's a story of self-reflection and growth, written from the scars, not the open wounds. It's a story about normalizing mental health and self-help. It's a story for anyone who has ever felt like something wasn't right but was told (either explicitly or implicitly) not to "rock the boat." For anyone who is done hiding from who they're meant to be. For anyone who has felt stuck or lost. For anyone who has ever felt like they weren't enough.

Spoiler alert: you are more than enough, just as you are. I've realized if we keep following the things that light us up, we'll never be stuck or lost again. Everything we need to feel whole is already inside of us. An inner voice, just waiting to lead the way.

I'm so glad you're here. I'm honored you've chosen to join me on my journey. And I'm excited for this book to support you along yours. Now is the time to spread *your* wings and fly!

Much love,
Chandra

PART ONE:

THE LEARNING

"A deep sense of love and belonging is an irreducible need of all people. We are biologically, cognitively, physically, and spiritually wired to love, to be loved, and to belong. When those needs are not met, we don't function as we were meant to. We break. We fall apart. We numb. We ache."

—BRENÉ BROWN

"If you don't heal the wounds of childhood, you bleed into the future."

—OPRAH WINFREY

CHAPTER 1

Unable to agree upon the moniker I would carry for the rest of my life (Jennifer and Nicole were the front runners), my parents opened a 1977 baby book of names to a random page and pointed.

"Chandra! It means moon in Sanskrit. She shines brighter than the stars," my dad announced excitedly.

"It's perfect," replied my mom with her signature beaming smile.

Named via random pointing, I think I got pretty lucky. Although I've spent forty-four years correcting others on its pronunciation ("it's a soft 'ch' like champagne or chandelier," I always say), only recently have I felt that maybe they chose it for a reason. It's like someone or something knew I'd have trouble finding my inner light and wanted my name to be a constant reminder of what I was meant to do in this world: shine brightly.

Shining brightly certainly didn't come naturally. The lessons I learned in early childhood shaped the adult I became, and then eventually, unbecame. Because that's what childhood is, right? One long stretch of conditioning. It's how we learn how to behave. It's when we begin to craft the masks we'll wear well into adulthood. Whether it be family, peers, teachers, or our community, the other people in our lives shape who we become. Other people's beliefs condition our own.

It's an uncertain time and there's no user manual. Today, I like to think I'm a great mom. A devoted mom, who wants her boys to develop strong emotional intelligence and social skills. To become brave and kind men. But the truth is, I've conditioned them with my own biases. Ideas they will need to unpack as adults and determine what they truly believe.

Much of the conditioning I underwent as a child in the 1980s was to be seen and not heard. And then, in some cases, not even seen. So, I developed coping mechanisms. Like making myself small and quiet. Like putting aside my wants and needs to make life easier for everyone else. Like dimming *my* light so *others* could shine more brightly.

In fact, I learned this early on, in the basement bedroom of my dad's new house. A place where my desperate need for sleep and safety were drowned out by an insect cacophony outside.

***

CRICKETS

One of my first vivid memories was the crickets. The way they chirped in the bush just outside my bedroom window, like thousands of tiny wailing banshees. I never understood why they sounded so loud. It's like they had nestled inside my pillow. Inside my brain.

I hated the crickets. Their relentless song made me feel anxious and uncomfortable. I feared they would come through the wall, and hundreds, thousands of jumping little legs would cover me, and I'd never come up for air. I was so terrorized, I believed I would suffocate under a blanket of chirping insects.

The crickets started after my dad left. I was six years old, and Dad moved out of the house he shared with Mom and me into a house he shared with his new wife, Demi, and her sons, my two new stepbrothers. My room was in the basement.

My only window, small and high on the stark white wall, was covered outside by bushes teeming with crickets.

I remember one specific night when I couldn't sleep. The crickets' screeching seemed even louder than usual and my adrenaline was pumping. I tiptoed upstairs and stood in the hallway outside my dad's bedroom. I hesitantly knocked on the door and heard stirring on the other side. There was grumbling and then heavy feet hit the wood floor. My annoyed father swung open the door, wearing only a pair of unbuttoned jeans thrown on haphazardly and a scowl.

"What?" he hissed. "What do you want?"

Looking back as a parent myself now, I'm sure he was just falling asleep, irritated to have been woken up. Or maybe he and his new wife were being intimate and I ruined a moment. Whatever the reason for this reaction, the only thing that made sense to my six-year-old brain was that I did something wrong. I froze in fear, wanting to turn and run, but more afraid of the crickets than my inconvenienced father.

"I'm scared. The crickets, they're so loud. I can't sleep," I said.

Now, if one of my boys said this to me, any momentary annoyance would have disappeared and my empathetic nature would kick in. I would want to protect them and make them feel better. I would lay down with them in their beds and turn the cricket sounds into a game. "Name that tune!" I might suggest, and we'd snuggle up. My little boys would fall asleep to the security of their mother's support and love.

But I am not my father. And at this time in our lives, he was not this kind of parent.

I'll be honest; I don't remember the exact words he said. If I were to paraphrase, it was something along the lines of "that's crazy, go back to bed" or "don't be a baby, they're just crickets. They're outside and can't get to you."

His response was not reassuring to my little brain and instead, I felt stupid and ashamed. Sorry for bothering Dad and still too scared to sleep in my bed.

Down to the dark cold living room, I shuffled. Onto the scratchy gray couch, I curled up. I was one floor below my dad and one floor above my room and those damned crickets. Far enough away from both I finally felt safe enough to sleep.

I often think back to that night and picture my little six-year-old self curled up on the couch. Breathing gently, but fraught with tension. If I could, I would pull her into my now-adult arms and cradle her. I would tell her she had done nothing wrong. I would calm her fears and make sure she knew she was loved.

When I go there in my mind, tears stream freely down my cheeks. Six-year-old Chandra is innocent. She is fragile, and I just want her to know she is safe. I wonder what my life would look like now if my dad had shared some of that reassurance? If I grew up knowing my emotions were valid and I was loved unconditionally? That she and me and all of us are allowed to be afraid of the crickets.

I soon discovered, however, these noisy insects were the least of my worries in Dad's new family.

EGGSHELLS

For the first six years of my life, I was the brightest star shining in my dad's sky. Everything revolved around me. I remember cuddling on our tan velour sofa (hey, it was the late 1970s) and him telling me stories he made up—harrowing tales about ordinary household objects. How the curtains and the coffee table were best friends. How the bookcase and the toaster had inside jokes. Whatever items I chose, he would create a story on the spot, and I was enamored. I felt loved and safe with my dad, which is why it was such a shock to my system when he left.

He had been having an affair and married his new wife less than five months after he moved out. He didn't fight for custody. He was starting a new life and I would be a part of it every other weekend.

The first time I met my stepmother Demi, I was a shy six-year-old whose world had just come crashing down. Her daddy had just moved out, her mommy was sad, and her own heart ached. So, when I was instructed to hug and kiss Demi upon our first meeting, my body tensed, and I wanted to run. Cropped black hair and porcelain skin, her appearance differed so strikingly from the soft brown curls of my tanned mom. She was a stranger, yet now had the word "mother" in a title related to me. I had no idea how to behave.

Honestly, it was no wonder—her moods were volatile. One moment she'd be laughing and singing and the next she'd be screaming and throwing things. In the beginning, it scared me. I'd run to my room and hide under the covers. Walking on eggshells became a talent I perfected.

I would later find out she had bipolar disorder, defined as "a mental illness characterized by dramatic shifts in mood and behavior." (*Self,* 2018)

"Scientists are still investigating the roots of the disorder, but they have identified three risk factors that contribute to your likelihood of developing the condition... genetics, brain structure and functioning, and family history." (*Self,* 2018)

I know now that Demi grew up in a tumultuous household with an abusive mother. She was the recipient of unresolved trauma, but to the mind of a child, it was all very confusing. I didn't understand why one day Demi would want to take me shopping and introduce me to her favorite movies. Historical dramas were her favorite—movies like *Amadeus* and *Dangerous Liaisons* left me feeling sophisticated and suddenly European.

Then the next day, she wouldn't speak to me. She'd walk right past me like I wasn't even there. I always felt on edge, like the next words out of my mouth might activate a tripwire. This could culminate in a screaming episode, or the cold shoulder. Both were equally terrifying.

I became anxious about everything when I was at my dad's house. When I greeted Demi, did I do it with enough excitement? If not, she'd say I didn't want to see her. Did I ask her enough questions about her week? If not, she'd claim I didn't really care about her. Did I compliment her on something—anything? If not, the explosives were triggered, and everything went up in flames.

One specific incident took place when I was eight years old. It was a Friday evening, just after I'd arrived at Dad and Demi's house. I turned on the TV and plopped down on the couch. I hadn't yet taken off my shoes (one of the rules in their house) as I was engrossed in a new episode of *Diff'rent Strokes*. I absentmindedly pulled one of my legs up underneath me.

At the exact same moment, Demi came into the room. The look of anger on her face tore my attention away from the drama on TV to the real-life drama about to unfold. I sat still and quiet, trying to prepare myself for the onslaught, but I had no idea what I had done. Had I not shown enough excitement when I first saw her? I thought I had, but maybe it wasn't enough. I began to silently chide myself for not doing more.

"What are you doing? WHAT ARE YOU DOING?" she screamed. "Get your fucking feet off of my furniture! Were you raised in a barn? What is wrong with you?"

I froze, looked down, and realized that indeed, the foot I was sitting on still wore its scuffed Reebok. I slowly lowered my foot, eyeing her as if she was a wild animal ready to pounce and I was her prey.

"I'm sorry," I said quietly.

But the blitz had only just begun. Another tirade of insults flew at me like shrapnel from an explosion. I've blocked out a lot of the specifics, but I do remember wishing I could roll myself into the tiniest ball and slip between the couch cushions, just so the screaming would stop.

Instead, I sat there in stunned silence until she turned around and ran out of the room. I heard the front door slam once, and then twice, as my father ran out after her.

She continued to yell and scream out in the cul-de-sac as I scurried up to my room. I have no idea what the neighbors thought, but if they were anything like me, they crawled under their covers and braced for it to be over.

Then the house was eerily quiet. My dad must have somehow calmed her down, and so began the depressive phase of bipolarism. The calm after the storm that was anything but. The static electricity of this phase was almost scarier.

I must have fallen asleep in my cocoon under the covers because the next thing I knew, it was morning. I carefully crept downstairs to pour myself a bowl of Cap'n Crunch. I hoped I could sneak in and out of the kitchen without being noticed. Unfortunately, my dad was sitting at the table, staring off into space with nothing but the sound of the clock ticking on the wall to break the silence.

He looked at me with an expression I didn't recognize. Looking back, his face was one of a defeated man. One who had just waged a bloody battle and lost. This man sitting in front of me looked sadder than I'd ever seen him before.

"I need you to apologize to her," he said rather matter-of-factly. A war-torn soldier stating the next steps for his platoon.

"What? Why?" I asked incredulously. "I didn't do anything."

"You know how she is. It will just make everything worse if you don't," he sighed with his eyes closed.

"Daddy, I'm not saying I'm sorry. I had my shoe on the couch for a minute. It was an accident," I pleaded.

Then his eyes filled up and the hopelessness behind them was more than my eight-year-old heart could take.

"Please, Chandra. For me, please apologize."

His tears flowed and my resolve diminished. It didn't seem fair I had to endure the repercussions of generational trauma that didn't even belong to me, but I couldn't stand to see my dad like this.

I went to her room where she was lying in bed, motionless. The heavy scent of her Opium perfume hung in the air.

"I'm really sorry for having my shoe on the couch. It won't happen again," I said.

She looked up at me slowly and a smile spread across her face. "Come and give me a hug, sweetheart," she whispered, and so I did as I was told.

I wish I could say occurrences like these were few and far between, but I would be lying.

I could have confided in my mom, but I never did. I could have told her that I didn't want to go back there, that I didn't feel safe, but I still hadn't learned how to give voice to my needs. Two years later, Dad and Demi had a son. I loved my little brother so much and if I'm honest, he was the real reason I continued to subject myself to the trauma every other weekend.

It took my dad twenty years to finally leave, but the damage was already done. I had perfected the art of people-pleasing and allowing myself to be manipulated. Those heavy feelings of worry and dread became my playmates. Anxiety became my constant babysitter.

SANCTUARIES
Over the years, I learned that if I don't ask for help and just apologize, the grown-ups will be happy regardless of whether I've done anything wrong. If I don't shine brightly, people will just leave me alone.

I lived with my mom most of the time, and although she was there for me emotionally, she was often absent physically. She worked several jobs and went to school most evenings so, usually, I was on my own from the time I got home from school until the time I went to bed.

I learned if I hid in my room under the covers and read, I could escape to other lives. Other families. Other worlds. It was quiet under there—still, like a sanctuary—and books were all I needed for nourishment.

As a latchkey kid in the 1980s, I had a lot of freedom and loved to pass the time finding new sanctuaries. My favorite was in our basement—I'd compile random items, sliding them together on the cold cement floor. Boxes of Christmas decorations, worn out from years of being taped up, opened, and then taped up again. My old brown plastic rocking horse, coated in dust. All of the various bits and bobs of our family history. Then over this motley crew of items, I'd spread the giant pink and purple quilt my grandmother had made for me when I was a baby.

Underneath the quilt, I'd lay more blankets and pillows. I added a Smurfs sleeping bag, my Cabbage Patch Dolls, and other favorite stuffed animals. I'd snuggle in there with my books, and nobody could bother me. In my sanctuary, it was just me and the words on the pages.

I traveled to Oz under my quilt. To Narnia. To witness a little girl named Margaret talk to God. To observe a group of friends navigate the turbulent waters of babysitting.

I learned that if I hid quietly in my sanctuary, I couldn't disappoint anyone. But, most importantly, no one could disappoint me.

As I got older, my sanctuaries transformed. Music became a new one. I'd spend hours on the cream-colored shag carpeting in my room listening to my mom's old 45s. I would stretch out, gazing at my lavender-painted walls covered with posters of Corey Haim, singing along with Jefferson Airplane and Peter, Paul and Mary.

The first album my mom bought me was Madonna's *Like a Virgin*. I was eight and had no idea what a virgin was, but I wanted to be a material girl all the same. Like books, music allowed me to explore worlds outside the one I lived in. I couldn't yet trust my own voice, so I mimicked the voices of others. My hunger for new music became insatiable.

I remember praying one night on my knees next to my bed, hands clasped together, and eyes squeezed tight in concentration.

"Dear God, please watch over my mom and me and all of my family and friends. Please watch over everyone else in the whole wide world. Please keep us safe and protect us. Oh, and, if you have time, please let my mom buy me the new Cyndi Lauper record. Amen."

And then, of course, there was TV. The 1980s were a golden age of television. Classic sitcoms like *Who's the Boss?*, *Growing Pains*, and *The Facts of Life* were as integral a part of my childhood as learning the truth about Santa Claus and getting chicken pox.

After finishing my homework, I'd heat up a Hungry-Man frozen dinner (my favorites were the ones with the brownie for dessert) and settle down in front of the tube for hours. I learned about the nuclear family from the Huxtables and the Keatons. I learned about my period from tampon commercials. I learned about homosexuality from *Three's Company* (thanks Mr. Roper). I learned about stranger danger from every "very special" episode and after-school special.

My mom tells me now, as an adult, I pretty much raised myself. But I don't see it this way. Books raised me. Music raised me. TV raised me.

My sanctuaries doubled as my classrooms. I escaped, *and* I learned about life at the same time. But, by far, the most surprising sanctuary I discovered was at the mall, among the mannequins.

MANNEQUINS

My relationship with my mom was very special. In contrast to being at my dad's house, being with Mom felt safe. I knew her love was unconditional and solid. She was my home base, but she was busy.

To keep the house after my dad left, she was always working. Her standard Monday through Friday nine to five was as a special education teacher in a rough Maryland county. Third graders brought knives to school. Fourth graders threatened to beat her up. I can't imagine the intense stress she must have been under. She commuted two hours each way and feared for her safety all day long.

Then, on the weekends, she worked odd jobs. She led divorce support groups at the local Women's Resource Center.

She worked as a receptionist for a CPA. She helped tutor at Sylvan Learning Center. She was even an Omaha Steak model. Dressed to the nines, she would stand in various high-end grocery stores, encouraging people to purchase the beautifully wrapped steaks. My mother would do whatever she needed to keep my life as normal as possible. If that's not love, I don't know what is.

One odd job I remember clearly was a perfume spritzer at Macy's. Every Saturday, off to the local mall we went. She would spritz and I would play. Macy's became my personal playground. For kids who've ever fantasized about getting locked in a store overnight (me!), this was the next best thing.

I was a responsible kid, so I would wear my watch and be sure to check in with her every hour. Those sixty minutes of freedom helped shape my independence into what it is today. I'd find little nooks in the department store and cozy up with a book. People watching became a favorite pastime, and occasionally, when I felt especially imaginative, I'd make up games.

Sometimes, I would pretend carousels of blouses were spaceships. I'd hide inside, waiting for the aliens (i.e., middle-aged women) to approach. I'm sure some poor unsuspecting customers were startled by the little blonde girl hiding in the clothing rack, but hey, it was the eighties. People minded their own business.

My favorite game was mannequins. Yes, it's just what you might think. I would stand on a pedestal and pretend I was one of the mannequins. In my seven-year-old mind, I *was* a mannequin. I would tense every muscle in my body and stand as still as I possibly could for as long as I possibly could.

Customers would walk by and smile. I thought they were smiling because I was such a realistic mannequin and was doing my job so well. I assumed one couldn't help but spontaneously smile at this season's latest fashion (I was most likely wearing my "uniform" of acid wash jeans and a Strawberry Shortcake sweatshirt).

Looking back, it's more likely they were smiling at the innocence of a little girl. A kid who was just being a kid. She was not afraid of what people thought because she was so confident in her ability to *be* a mannequin.

The respite and independence my mother gave me on those Saturdays at Macy's was such a gift, one I still treasure to this day. It allowed me to stretch my creative muscles, all while feeling the safety net of my mom, who was only a few yards away. It was an escape where I got to control the narrative of my reality for a few hours. It was an opportunity to explore different parts of myself.

I learned that sometimes, pretending to be someone or something else was an effective way to figure out who I actually was: someone who could shine brighter than the stars.

CHAPTER 2

On the outside, I seemed like a regular kid. I got good grades. I was polite and considerate. Teachers, parents, and other kids all seemed to like me. As I shuffle through old photos, I see a little girl with a gap-toothed smile and squinty eyes (an early sign of needing glasses). She looks happy.

But under the surface, anxiety boiled, churned, and sloshed against my insides like a sailboat caught in rough ocean waters.

I always worried about what others thought. In friendships, I always felt like I got the better end of the deal. I was sure another person could somehow improve my existence in ways I'd never be able to reciprocate. So, I'd secretly obsess over the fact I *knew* they were cooler, prettier, smarter, or more athletic than me.

Who was I to make their life better?

What did I have to offer?

Although I was funny, loyal, and a good listener, I never felt like I was enough. I was always waiting for the other shoe to drop. Then, when someone inevitably decided they didn't want to be my friend any longer, I could wallow in the fact I knew I was right. No story illustrates this more than my friendship with Katie.

***

BFFS

I met Katie in the eighth grade. Paired up as science lab partners, we connected almost instantly. Her warm brown eyes matched her warm brown hair and her smile was as infectious as it was genuine. She became the kind of best friend who feels more like a long-lost sister. Once we met, it was hard to remember life before her. We became extensions of each other.

Katie lived in an upper-middle-class suburb with two married parents, a little brother, and a poodle. In my memory, her house had a white picket fence, but I could be projecting. You get the picture, though. She had the normalcy and stability I craved.

I loved being at her house and slept over often. Her mom would cook baked ziti and we'd watch movies in her basement. We'd put on fashion shows, talk about which boys we thought were cute, and listen to cassettes of our favorite bands. She was pretty and popular and had this sense of self-confidence I admired. She had everything I'd ever wanted, and I felt so lucky she'd chosen to share her light with me.

The school year passed, along with summer, and suddenly, we were in high school. Both still navigating the cliques and various groups, trying to figure out where we fit in, we decided to try out for cheerleading. So, for a few hours a day, older (read: cooler) girls instructed us on various jumps and cheers and choreographed a dance number to the Deee-Lite song, "Groove Is in the Heart."

We practiced every day after school. Her herkies and high kicks were better than mine, but I was determined. Finally, tryouts day came, and I gave it my all. I knew I wasn't as agile as some of the other girls, but I hoped they'd give me a shot.

I didn't make the squad, but Katie did.

I was bummed about me, but genuinely happy for her. I figured at least one of us had found her place in this overwhelmingly huge school and my turn would be next.

It was 1991 and during this time, I started to experiment with my wardrobe. I was drawn to skateboarding culture and began dressing accordingly. I wore baggy jeans and skater shoes like Etnies and Airwalks. Grunge was taking off and flannel shirts became permanently tied around my waist.

Although Katie and I were starting to dress a little differently, we were still the same people. We still laughed in her basement at inside jokes, wrote each other notes, and passed them to each other between classes—until it changed.

The notes stopped. The inside jokes stopped. It had been weeks since I'd been to Katie's house. And then one day we were walking down the crowded high school hallway, and through saccharine sweetness, she said under her breath, "Chandra, if you're going to walk down the hall with me while I'm wearing my cheerleading uniform, you have to smile."

I was shocked. This comment was so unlike anything I'd heard from her before. I joked, "Are you serious?"

Katie looked me directly in the eyes and said, with no irony, "Yes. It is very important that I maintain a certain image now."

My heart dropped into my stomach and the familiar feeling of wanting to hide returned. But, like I had done so many times before with my stepmother, I just whispered, "Okay," and kept going.

After that day, things were never the same. She stopped calling me. She stopped making eye contact in the halls. Soon, we were strangers in a mass of high school freshmen.

I took down all the photos of us I had in my room. Deflated mylar balloons Katie got me for my birthday sunk to the floor. I threw them away along with a welcome home sign she made me after I returned from a trip out west. She was my first real heartbreak. It was yet another lesson in how situations can change overnight and how people can leave and never look back. It was the catalyst for years of trying to figure out who I really was.

PHASES

After my friendship with Katie ended, I felt lost. I didn't know who I was apart from her. So, I revived the lesson I learned as a mannequin in Macy's all those years before. If I pretended to be somebody else, people would smile. This ignited a series of phases I went through in high school, all in an attempt to figure out who I really was.

The skateboarding phase evolved in sophomore year when I only wore clothes from thrift stores and my grandmother's closet. Her polyester butterfly collar blouses paired perfectly with my "vintage" wide-leg Rustler jeans and old skate shoes. The hole-ridden pilled sweaters and baggy corduroys from the Salvation Army hung off my skinny frame. My self-esteem was at a low point and I didn't think of myself as pretty. So, I hid behind this uniform thinking it protected me.

My long blonde hair continuously got shorter and I dyed it a strawberry blonde (read: orange). Being "alternative" became my identity and I hoped it communicated to the outside world not to mess with me. Feel free to love me, but you won't get close enough to leave me.

Glennon Doyle Melton shares her experience in *Love Warrior* as such: "Every morning before I walk into high school I tell myself, *Just hold your breath 'til you get home.* I throw back my shoulders, smile, and walk into the hallway like a superhero in a cape. To onlookers it appears that I've finally found myself. I haven't, of course. What I've found is a representative of me who's just tough and trendy enough to survive high school. The magic of sending my representative is that the real me cannot be hurt." (Melton, 2016)

Side note: Glennon and I went to high school together, so maybe it was just us? I don't know, but feigning self-confidence to survive the day was very much a survival skill I had to master to stay afloat in a school with over 4,000 teenagers.

Eventually, the baggy used clothes phase morphed into a more feminine version of "alternative." My fashion idol at the time was Drew Barrymore. She inspired me to wear baby doll dresses with combat boots and colorful plastic barrettes to secure my blunt bob. I copied her dark lipstick and thin eyebrows, choker necklaces, and platform shoes.

I had started working at the mall in a store called Georgetown Cotton. It was the best mix of hippy and club kid clothes, shoes, and accessories. We sold gauzy skirts and peasant blouses, as well as Doc Martens and Manic Panic hair dye. By senior year, my skirts had gotten shorter as my confidence had gotten stronger. I was still "alternative," but now "sexy" was an identity I was exploring.

A virgin who had never done more than kiss a boy was now eschewing baggy sweaters for crop tops. Showing more skin was something that made me feel stronger. I instinctively knew boys (and probably some creepy older men) started to see me differently. I liked the power it inspired and though I never acted on it physically, the new possibilities of what I *could* do were intoxicating.

I had also found a new best friend named Alex. Or rather, she found me. Paired up as science lab partners (oh the irony!) our junior year, she complimented me on my baby barrettes and I on her Phish t-shirt. She was the opposite of Katie. Popular and pretty, yes, but constantly pushing boundaries. Her tight blonde curls and sharp tongue reminded me of a

Shirley Temple gone bad. Smoking cigarettes and skipping school were her favorite pastimes. She was voted "Most Likely to Fall Asleep in Class" in senior superlatives. We both felt like outcasts and for the first time in so long, I felt seen.

Experimentation was something I was now open to beyond just my fashion choices. In 1995, the rave scene was at its height of popularity and both Alex and I were inexplicably drawn to it. Maybe it was the dark crowded rooms where you could blend into the crowd. Maybe it was because everyone there wore a costume (literally and figuratively). Or maybe, it was the drugs.

The first time I snuck out and went to a rave, I felt like I had found my "thing." Alex and I had decided I'd spend a Thursday night at her house since it was easier to sneak out on her mom than mine. After driving ninety minutes to Baltimore, a group of us stood outside on the "patio" of an abandoned warehouse, put a tiny piece of inky paper on our tongues, and waited for the LSD to kick in. We knew it had when a giant billboard for the Hair Cuttery started moving. The man in the photo, who only moments before had been completely still, began running his hand through his hair.

Suddenly, everything around me changed. Colorful waves began cascading from each corner of what had been a dingy concrete building just moments before. I could actually *see* the loud vibrating dance music in the air, like a thousand bursts of light moving in unison. All the faces that had previously seemed unknown and scary became beautiful and friendly, like I'd known them forever. All I felt was an intense love for myself and my fellow humans.

After dancing until the wee hours of the morning, driving home, and sneaking back into Alex's house, we got dressed and went to school. This became routine for the two of us, sneaking up to Baltimore at least twice a month for the rest of our senior year.

Graduation came and the last summer before college was here. Alex and I pierced our noses and our tongues. We continued to attend raves, but at some point, the LSD evolved to ecstasy, which evolved to ketamine, and eventually, cocaine.

The beautiful colors and emotions I'd initially experienced with drugs had dimmed to a dark gritty harshness. I weighed ninety-seven pounds. I was disappearing. An environment that once felt like home now started to feel like a giant black hole.

I was being swallowed up in a world I had no business being in—a cold world of paranoia, where everyone had a secret agenda, and searching for the next buzz was their only goal. And then, I finally hit rock bottom.

One afternoon, a friend and I were bored, so she called a guy she knew to buy some ecstasy. Moments after we swallowed our pills, I asked her how she knew this guy.

"He's an ex-boyfriend. I'm actually surprised he sold it to us. He kind of hates me," she shared.

Oh shit.

PATTERNS

We had been driving around and both suddenly felt sick. We pulled over to lie down on a patch of grass in the parking lot of an apartment complex. We didn't vacate that patch of grass for *seven hours*. Each time one of us would attempt to move, overwhelming nausea would take over. It felt like I was going to throw up my entire body, inside out, and all that would be left of me was a puddle of a girl with questionable decision-making skills.

I'm still shocked nobody called the police on two girls lying motionless in the parking lot for so long. When we finally regained control of our bodies, we got back in the car and drove back to my friend's house. She immediately called her ex and demanded to know what he had given us.

I could hear him laughing on the other end of the line. Heroin. He had sold us pills of heroin.

In one distinct moment, as the horror of what could have transpired hit me, I realized then and there my drug phase was now over. Unlike so many of the people I hung out with, I knew I had a bright future ahead of me. I had been accepted into college and I wasn't going to screw it up. A new beginning was waiting for me.

In a matter of days, I began shedding the skin that no longer fit me. I let go of all the toxic relationships in my life and was again at a point where I had no friends. Unlike what happened with Katie, this time *I* was the one who decided to walk away, but I still felt alone and abandoned. Maybe it was because my former "friends" didn't seem to care I stopped hanging out with them.

Or maybe it was because I realized I had been abandoning *myself* just to fit in for years.

I opened up to my mom during this challenging time. She was my biggest support system and, of course, had noticed the rapid weight loss and mood changes. She'd expressed her concern, but since I was now eighteen and technically an adult, she had little control over my behavior. She knew if she pushed me to change, then I'd only push back harder.

So instead of forcing ultimatums, she calmly shared her fears for me if I continued down the road I was on. She made sure I understood she would be there when I needed her. She continued to be my home base, knowing I'd eventually return. She was, and still is, my rock of unwavering support.

Looking back, I believe she intuitively trusted I would figure myself out. She had witnessed the many phases of her daughter and had faith I'd find myself eventually. And it's true; I began to notice patterns in my behavior. I started asking myself important questions.

Why was I always looking for a way to hide from the world?

Why was I always trying on different identities to figure out who I was?

As I've dived deeper into personal development in my adult life, I've read that low self-esteem and self-destructive habits like drug use can often be linked to abandonment trauma in early childhood.

In *What Happened to You*, a book about trauma, resilience, and healing written by Bruce D. Perry and Oprah Winfrey, Perry states, "What I've learned from talking to so many victims of traumatic events, abuse, or neglect is that after absorbing these painful experiences, the child begins to ache. A deep longing to feel needed, validated, and valued begins to take hold. As these children grow, they lack the ability to set a standard for what they deserve. And if that lack is not addressed, what often follows is a complicated, frustrating pattern of self-sabotage, violence, promiscuity, or addiction." (Perry and Winfrey, 2021)

All I ever wanted was to belong, but it seemed just out of reach, even among the people I loved the most.

My dad, whose job was to love and support me, abandoned me to start a new life—one in which I felt I didn't belong. He chose his new wife's emotional well-being over that of his young daughter's. He dismissed and denied my genuine childhood fears. That, combined with my stepmother's erratic behavior, pushed me to retreat further into my personal sanctuaries.

I was lucky to be able to depend emotionally on my mom, but physically, she was rarely there. And although I finally found a sense of belonging with Katie, losing it once I had a taste was almost worse than never knowing what it was like in the first place.

What is the opposite of belonging? Alienation. How did I survive? By hiding from the chaos. I was unable to trust other people, so I hid. As a young child, I hid behind books and music and TV. As I got older, I hid behind different identities and, eventually, behind drugs.

Now, in limbo between childhood and adulthood, about to head off into a new world, I knew it was an opportunity for a fresh start. I no longer identified with any of my previous phases. I discarded them as I entered a new chapter of life.

Still aching for somewhere to belong, I vowed my time in college would be well spent. This time, I'd finally figure out who I really was and find others like me. I'd merge with my tribe of like-minded souls. I had such high hopes and naive expectations.

Little did I know that instead of finding my truth, I'd simply be trading in one mask for another and discovering new ways to hide.

CHAPTER 3

In my continued effort to belong, I decided to change course. Instead of trying to be different in college, I'd try to fit in. Mind-blowing, I know.

I had always been the girl pushing "normal" people away with my look and lifestyle, but this time, I was going to move in the opposite direction. I began studying what the other girls at my liberal arts college in Virginia were wearing and doing. I got a job at American Eagle. I dyed my hair back to its original blonde. I removed my nose and tongue rings.

And it worked. I started making new friends. Keg parties and cheering at soccer games became my new hobbies outside of class. I started having the "conventional" college experience—parties, weekend camping trips, and dancing in dorm rooms. Finally, I felt like I fit in. I was enjoying life again, this time without drugs. Inevitably though, since I still hadn't healed the original abandonment wounds, I soon traded one bad habit for another.

***

ISLANDS

Boys had never really been interested in me in high school. At least, not that I knew. I spent so much time trying to keep people at a distance that even if someone had a crush on me, I would have been oblivious. So, when boys in college started noticing me, it all felt very new and exciting.

I had finally lost my virginity the summer before college and felt like I had reached a new level of womanhood. Coupled with the liquid courage of alcohol, I honed my flirting skills and began to relish advances from the opposite sex.

Intoxicated with attention and Milwaukee's Best, the boys plus the booze were beginning to equal a sense of belonging, even if only for a night.

Young and attractive with nothing to lose, I tried on different guys like I was shopping for jeans at The Gap (it was the late nineties and nobody did denim better). Lots of parties, lots of making out. The trifecta of vodka, cute guys, and lowered inhibitions put a wrench in my ability to make good choices. Most of the time, the casual encounters provided me with a hangover and a funny story.

But not spring break my junior year. One night changed me in ways I'm still processing to this day.

It was 1998, and a group of us went to St. Thomas for a week of sun and fun. We'd shop and hit the beach during the day and take the ferry over to the island of St. John at night. We discovered a watering hole for locals early on in our trip and made an appearance nightly.

The bartenders knew us and gave us free drinks. Several Americans were living temporarily on the island and we'd become friendly with a group of them. One was Philip from South Carolina. He was spending a year on St. John waiting tables and living his best life, all on his daddy's dime. He had some pretentious four-word name which definitely ended with "the third." He simultaneously annoyed me with his pompousness and made me laugh.

One night, a group of us met at the bar and then hit some clubs. Of the four girls I was with, two had the sense to head back to the ferry in time to make the last boat to St. Thomas.

Unfortunately, I was not one of them. So, I asked Philip if I could crash on his couch. He said it was fine and we stumbled off. As soon as we made it to his apartment, I ran to the bathroom. I was in there for a solid twenty minutes throwing up my dinner and what felt like gallons of Cruzan rum.

When I came out, Philip was there and said I could sleep in his bed. He said it was no big deal. At that point in the night, I was so out of it, he could have pointed me in the direction of a bathtub and I would have happily crawled inside. Instead, I collapsed into his bed and started to pass out.

Until I felt him climb on top of me.

He grabbed and tore at my underwear, the white ones with the red flowers. I told him I didn't want to do that. I said, "NO." I repeated it over and over, but he didn't listen. He forced his way inside of me, and luckily, I blacked out.

When I woke up the next morning, he wasn't beside me. I lay there, slowly trying to remember the night before. Fuzzy images began to sharpen and an overwhelming sense of disgust washed over me.

A wave of nausea hit, and I raced to the bathroom. Tears streamed down my face from both the violent vomiting and last night's memories, which began to rush back. I walked out of the bathroom to get my shoes and saw Philip asleep on the porch in a hammock.

I fought the urge to shove him out of his blissful sleep and onto the hard ground. And although I glared at him with intense hatred and disgust, I simultaneously choked back tears and shame. I figured what had happened was somehow my fault.

I quietly left his apartment and walked down to the dock. I caught the ferry back to St. Thomas, snuck into the hotel room where my friends were still passed out, and crawled under the covers. I cried as silently as I could until they began to stir. The other girl who had gotten stuck on St. John came back in similar shape to me. We never talked about what happened.

I finally told one of the girls about my experience over a year later. We were at a party and I pulled her aside.

"Hey Melissa, do you remember those guys we met in St. John?" I asked nonchalantly.

"Oh my gosh, *yes*! They were so fun!" she responded enthusiastically.

"I need to tell you what really happened. One of them sexually assaulted me the night I didn't come back with you on the ferry," I said quietly while I studied the contents of my red Solo cup.

I looked up and saw her staring at me with wide eyes and an open mouth.

Before she could respond, I continued quickly, "I don't know why I didn't tell you before. I think I was embarrassed because I know I should have left when you did. I should have stopped drinking rum and started drinking water. I've been blaming myself for so long and I just needed to tell someone."

Melissa reached over and hugged me tightly. "None of this was your fault, Chandra. I am so sorry this happened to you. I had no idea."

It took me years to call it what it was. Every time I tried, anxiety would roil in my stomach and I'd clamp my mouth shut.

Rape.

I was raped in St. John on spring break during my sophomore year in college.

I can say it now because I know it wasn't my fault. Philip Asshole Entitled Prick the Third could have left me alone. He could have made me a bed on the couch. He could have gotten me a glass of water and fallen asleep on the other side of the bed. He could have made numerous choices that didn't involve him inserting his penis in me while I was fighting unconsciousness.

When I read a statistic that among undergraduate students, 26.4 percent of females experience rape or sexual assault, it didn't surprise me (RAINN, 2014). That's one-in- four-odds. Doubled with the fact that rape is the most under-reported crime—63 percent of sexual assaults are not reported to police (Rennison, 2002)—I realized I was not the exception. I was the rule. I could have reported it, but would anyone have believed me? Where was the proof it hadn't been consensual? At the time, I still hadn't admitted the truth to myself.

I hope wherever he is now, he thinks about those choices. I hope he thinks about how they affected the women he assaulted, because I'm sure I wasn't the first, or the last. Yes, I could have made better choices that night. But I didn't deserve what happened to me. I can see that now and I hope if you've experienced something similar, you can see that too.

We did nothing wrong. We do not have to feel ashamed any longer. None of this was our fault.

SCISSORS

Even though I understand now the rape wasn't my fault, my twenty-one-year-old self wasn't as wise and experienced. So, besides Melissa, I hadn't told anyone else what happened. I didn't even acknowledge it had taken place. Instead, I treated the entire experience like some low-rate film I'd watched and just wanted to forget.

The anxiety I felt since childhood ebbed and flowed throughout the different phases of my life. But, during my senior year in college, it came to a head. Not dealing with my emotions around the rape coupled with the fact I was about to graduate and didn't have a job lined up yet, I woke up in a panic each day.

Heart palpitations and shortness of breath greeted me each morning. My mind would race throughout the day, and I'd begin to sweat each time I realized I had no control over anything. My future. My past. Other people's expectations of me.

I would also keep a running tally of all the things I thought I should be doing but couldn't bring myself to accomplish. I had put on some weight, so I chided myself about not working out enough. Not eating healthily enough. Not being enough.

My study habits, which had once been systematic, were replaced by constant napping. My once vibrant social life became dull by my lack of interest in anything beyond my bed. And when the emotional pain became too intense and I couldn't sleep, I created a physical outlet.

I began cutting myself.

On the nights when I felt most alone and my fear was at its darkest, I opened my desk drawer and took out my scissors. Cutting the soft flesh of my inner arm deep enough to bleed but not enough to scar, I felt a release. It's like the blade immediately transformed the emotional pain into physical pain. Something I could name. Something I could see. Something I could manage. It allowed me to take back some control.

At the time, I had no idea this was something other people did too. It was 1999, so the media wasn't talking about it and the Internet was still in its infancy. It just felt natural to me, like scratching the most intense itch to provide the sweetest sigh of relief.

I wasn't doing it because I wanted to kill myself or for attention. In fact, I hid my arms so I wouldn't have to answer questions. I did it because it was the only thing that provided any relief.

The secret cutting went on for months. And then, one night, when even the physical pain wasn't enough, and the fear was deeper and darker than ever before, I called my mom. I don't remember my exact words, but I know they rushed out of my mouth in a hurricane of tears and hiccups and shame.

At the time, she was living in Ohio, 400 miles away from my school in Virginia. She thought my dad could help because geographically, he was closer, only two hours away in Maryland.

"I'm so sorry you're going through this. I want to be there for you, but I'm so far away. Is it okay if I call your dad?" she asked.

I shrugged and said, "Whatever."

I had been going to college just hours from where he lived for nearly four years and his visits were infrequent at best. Nevertheless, she called and asked him to come and check on me. As a mother myself now, she must have been terrified. It probably seemed like a cry for help. Maybe it was.

A couple of days later, on a sunny Saturday afternoon, my dad knocked on the door of the townhouse I shared with my roommate. After an awkwardly quiet ride to the local diner, we sat down in a sticky vinyl booth. The scent of fried foods wafted over us from the open kitchen doors.

More awkward silence ensued until finally, he blurted out, "So, are you trying to kill yourself?"

I sat with the heavy question hanging in the air for what seemed like hours but was likely only a few seconds. I wanted to answer honestly.

"No," I said. "No, I don't want to kill myself."

I felt my eyes begin to burn and then the tears started flowing.

I came very close to telling him about what had transpired in St. John, but I still felt such incredible shame and embarrassment around the situation. I couldn't bear the thought of going to him with this particular landmine and having it blow up in my face. If the crickets had taught me anything, it was to keep my mouth shut. So instead, I offered a generic response.

"I just feel sad, and I don't know why. I think maybe I need some help."

Looking back, this meeting might have been an opportunity to begin repairing our broken relationship. I could have been more honest about how I was feeling, but he could have dug a little deeper, tried a little harder to get to the truth. Instead, he accepted my words without any further questioning, and in turn, I reinforced my walls to keep my secret hidden from him.

He agreed I should talk to someone and when we got back to my place, he helped me find the phone numbers of some local therapists. One woman had availability the following week, so I made an appointment to meet with her.

Like the emotions I had before heading off to college for the first time, I felt hopeful a professional could finally help me find my truth. That someone could help me figure myself out so I could finally find a sense of peace.

TECHNIQUES

I met with Lisa on a cloudy Thursday afternoon. Her office sat in a strip mall, a multilevel brick building next to a tanning salon. As I perched nervously on the worn green sofa, all I could hear was the whirring of the noise machines built to keep conversations private from those in the waiting room. Then a door opened, and a middle-aged woman with frizzy auburn hair and kind eyes greeted me.

"Hi, I'm Lisa. You must be Chandra," she said with a warm smile.

This wasn't my first experience with a therapist. When my parents got divorced, I went to see Cindy. The only thing I remember about our sessions was playing board games while I sucked on sugar cubes from the coffee station. I wasn't sure what to expect with Lisa, but I noticed there weren't any sugar cubes or board games in sight.

I took my seat in a brown leather chair across from her and answered some preliminary questions—my age, where I went to school, and what I was studying. And then *the* question that's inevitably asked came: "So what brings you in today?"

I don't know what inspired me to unload onto Lisa. Maybe it was the way the buttery leather cushions held me and made me feel safe. Maybe it was the understanding behind her eyes and the way they crinkled when she smiled. Or maybe I had just been holding it all in for much too long.

I told Lisa everything. I described what had happened in St. John, the anxiety that had been exacerbated in the past year, and the cutting. She asked questions and offered genuine compassion.

"Have you ever heard of cognitive behavioral therapy?" she inquired.

"Cogni—what now?" I asked in my usual self-deprecating way.

She laughed and continued. "Cognitive behavioral therapy is a kind of talk therapy, like what we're doing now. As we talk, we start to find patterns in your thoughts about yourself and the world around you. And when we find a thought that may be hurting you, we find a way to change it."

It sounded almost too simple to work, like changing my thoughts was as easy as snapping my fingers. But as I've found in my forty-four years on this earth, just because something sounds simple, it doesn't mean it's easy. There is still work to do.

According to the American Psychological Association, many psychological problems are based in part "on unhelpful ways of thinking" or "learned patterns of unhelpful behavior." Cognitive behavioral therapy (CBT) usually involves efforts to change such thinking and behavioral patterns (APA, 2021).

Lisa taught me techniques to do just this.

The first was journaling. The power behind journaling is it can help you become consciously aware of negative thinking happening just below the surface, in the subconscious. That's where the juicy stuff lives.

Writing had always been something I enjoyed and creative writing was one of my favorite classes in high school. However, I hadn't done much writing in college and was excited to begin a regular journal practice. It's a tool I still use to this day to get thoughts out of my head and onto paper. Many of those words even made it into this book.

Another CBT technique I learned was reframing. Often, I would have all-or-nothing thinking. I would assume one thing *always* happens, whereas another thing *never* does. Becoming aware of this pattern, I started to stop myself in the moment and reframe the situation in my mind. I'd ask myself, does this thing really *always* or *never* happen, or can I think of times the outcome was different? Reframing is another tool I still use to this day and one that's allowed me to look at things from a new perspective.

After working with Lisa for a few months and starting on an antidepressant (God bless Zoloft), I finally felt like I was back at my baseline. I felt much more emotionally prepared to graduate college and enter the real world. The gray clouds hanging over my head for so long began to clear. I could take a deep breath without the weight of a baby elephant on my chest. I began to feel actual excitement for this new chapter. It's not an exaggeration for me to say therapy changed my life.

However, please don't think I was "fixed." I had learned new techniques to make being human a little easier, but I hadn't yet done the work to heal. As much as I'm a proponent of CBT, it doesn't deal with the past.

Cognitive behavioral therapy helped me focus on moving forward but didn't touch my childhood trauma. It improved my coping methods but didn't repair the original wounds.

Looking back, it acted as a much-needed Band-Aid, allowing me to step back into my humanness. Unfortunately, it would still be years before I'd begin the process of true healing.

CHAPTER 4

Adulting is not for the faint of heart. Not unlike my kids' laundry, it's unpredictable, overwhelming, and usually smelly. It doesn't do itself and I'm always surprised at how much of it there is.

Although my true healing work would come much later in life, the techniques I learned from Lisa allowed me to better navigate my twenties without falling apart (too often). Most of the time, I could catch myself in a negative thought spiral and re-right the ship before it lost control. Thanks to writing, therapy, and antidepressants, my anxiety was under control. I felt a tentative sense of hopefulness.

Even though I still had no idea what the future would bring, I was ready to move forward.

***

LADDERS

The classes I loved in college were always related to art, philosophy, or anthropology—anything that allowed me to see things in a new way. Maybe I was intrigued by my own life phases and patterns because I loved learning about different cultures and perspectives. I began dreaming about working in a museum. I wanted to educate people through the arts—introduce them to new worlds and ideas.

I majored in historic preservation with a minor in art history. My first job out of college was, indeed, as an educator at the Smithsonian Early Enrichment Center, SEEC for short. It was an education center for the children of Smithsonian employees and housed within the museums themselves. I worked in the Museum of Natural History, teaching tiny bright-eyed humans through historic relics and the arts. I loved the potential to shape young minds and the constant inspiration I gained from walking around museums all day.

I remember one specific day with the kindergarteners. We went to see a Piet Mondrian painting at the National Gallery of Art. Mondrian was a Dutch painter who expressed himself through the three primary colors (red, blue, and yellow) and only painted dark lines in two directions, horizontal and vertical.

I asked the class to study the image and share their reflections with the group.

"What do you think the artist is trying to show us?" I inquired.

A precocious little girl raised her hand and proceeded to inform me, "Well, it's kind of obvious, isn't it? It's a beach. The blue is the ocean, the yellow is the sand, and the red is the sunset."

Now, I want *you* to Google "Piet Mondrian neoplasticism" and let me know how obvious it is. Children see things through eyes so different than ours. It's incredibly magical to witness moments like this.

Another time, I took the class to view a piece by Jackson Pollock, a famous American abstract expressionist painter.

"How does this painting make you feel?" I asked my sweet little brood.

"Happy!" cried one little girl.

"Excited!" yelled another.

"Miss Kennett, this painting makes me feel very sad," said one little boy very quietly.

"Yes, I can feel all of those things when I look at this painting. How cool is it that we can experience all of these different emotions from some paint on a canvas?" I observed.

This event latched in my mind as an instance of pure innocence and vulnerability. The lessons we can learn from young people are astonishing. They all nodded and we moved on. Both of those days have stuck with me decades later, especially the honesty and bravery of their expanding minds. Nothing had brought me a feeling of joy and fulfillment in that way before and wouldn't again for a long time.

As adulthood makes painfully obvious, money makes the world go round. Making $18,000 a year (before taxes) did not allow me to live the kind of life I desired. I could barely afford my rent and commuted over two hours *each way* daily, just like my mother had over a decade before. It began to take its toll and I left after a year. Looking back, I realize the Smithsonian Early Enrichment Center was the first job that genuinely allowed me to be *me,* and I will always be grateful for the experience. "SEEC" and you shall find.

To save money and be close to my mom again, I decided to move to Cincinnati, Ohio. She had settled down there when I left for college and I had enjoyed my visits to the Queen City on school breaks. I found a job as an administrative assistant at a large tax firm and became friendly with the accountants who were my age. However, our working relationship soon spilled into out-of-office antics. We went out to clubs, concerts, and restaurants. Several of them lived in the same apartment complex so our weekend plans often consisted of pool parties and BBQs.

The biggest difference between us was that they had the funds to do these fun things. They were all making close to six figures only a few years out of college. In stark contrast, I was living with my mom and trying to keep up on an administrative assistant's wage of nothing close to that. So, when they wanted to take a trip to Las Vegas and I couldn't afford it, I decided I needed a change. I wanted to make more money so I could travel, drive a nice car, and buy cute clothes. Sign me up for the corporate ladder. Finally, a new way I could find a sense of belonging.

I applied for graduate school at the University of Cincinnati and was accepted into their one-year, full-time accelerated MBA program. I quit my job and buckled down for those twelve months, learning everything about business I'd never learned in undergrad. The classes that sparked my interest the most were related to marketing. It seemed like the closest thing to a creative outlet I would find in business. In addition to coming up with fun campaign ideas and clever taglines, I imagined an average day in my life as a marketer consisting of fancy cappuccinos and Banana Republic suits, racing from meeting to meeting and then martinis after work. Honestly, I wasn't far off.

MBA in hand, I was finally able to make some significant money. My first job with my master's degree was as a consumer insights manager. Researching flavor and fragrance trends for big brands scratched the itch of working in a creative environment and having my own cubicle. We had cute graphic designers and Friday happy hours. Yes, I realize my list of job requirements was questionable. I even remember one Cinco de Mayo; everyone got a Corona to drink at their desk during work hours. It was the perfect place for twenty-five-year-old me.

But after five years in the Midwest, I was homesick for the east coast. So, I moved back to Washington, DC in 2005 and started a job in media monitoring. It was nothing like my consumer insights job and I hated it. Today, if a company wants to collect all the articles written about it and sort for sentiment (i.e., if it's favorable or unfavorable), they just have to click a few buttons on a dashboard. Well, back then, *I* was the dashboard, and all sentiment was rated by hand—*my* hand. I had eleven clients for whom I monitored and rated media hits. Each day, I essentially read and graded articles and then wrote reports.

I had a personal goal of working there for one year and then I could look elsewhere. However, the silver lining of this monotonous job was that it became a stepping stone into public relations. One year later, I was offered an account executive position at a local PR agency specializing in crisis communications.

I loved it there. For the first time in my career, I felt important. I felt established. In some ways, I felt like this job let me open people's eyes to new ideas and experiences, while still allowing me to be creative. Not unlike a traveling museum exhibit, I was able to take a prototype of the Volt, Chevrolet's first electric car, on a roadshow to cities across the country.

My sweet spot in public relations was managing events. I think it was the mix of creating an educational and entertaining experience for people. And while I honed my event skills, a new group emerged in the agency. It was called New Media and led by a team of two who began following and sharing on something called Twitter. Around the same time, a platform called Facebook had just started allowing people without a college email address to have a profile. Blogs began to explode and brands were taking notice. I was poised right on the cusp of something huge.

PROPOSALS

I had just turned thirty, was killing it at work, and had just bought my first condo. I felt like I was checking off all the boxes I was supposed to. I relished my ability to adult. All the tools I'd learned years ago with Lisa had gotten me this far and while I still didn't 100 percent know who I was or what I wanted, I felt like I was getting closer.

One Friday night, I was out with some girlfriends at a DC bar. That particular evening, they were offering two-for-one cocktails, so the place was packed. Music thumping and drinks flowing, I sat on the couch with my friends, not looking for any romantic connection.

And then I met Adam.

Trucker hat and bright blue eyes, he had this endearing mix of bravado and vulnerability. His swagger and cocky smile conveyed confidence, while his baby face looked awestruck at all the excitement in the club.

When he sidled up behind my group of friends to talk to me, I asked him how old he was. He told me he was twenty-four. Then, in my most condescending voice, I turned and said, "Oh honey, I just don't think you're ready for the things I'm ready for."

"How do you know what I'm ready for?" he asked with a sly smirk.

I turned my head so he couldn't see my smile.

He then proceeded to ask my friend to dance. He spun her around the dance floor, showing off his smooth moves for my benefit. It worked. I cut in, we danced, and I was hooked. I found out later he called his mom that night and told her he'd met the girl he was going to marry.

We went on our first date the following week. Adam told me he didn't like seafood, but my favorite restaurant was Coastal Flats (read: they mostly have seafood). He sucked it up anyways and ordered the chicken. I think I was the first girl who challenged him, who didn't give in every time he flashed the grin that made all the girls melt. I think this is one of the reasons he fell so hard, so fast.

After our first date, everything moved quickly. We became inseparable and I all but moved into his apartment after only a few weeks. A couple of months later, I went with him to Boston to meet his family and rode with him as he drove his car back to Virginia, where we lived. Within ten months, we were engaged.

The proposal took place while we were vacationing on the Amalfi Coast in Italy. Adam and I took a late afternoon stroll through a garden in Ravello. He was acting nervous and I thought it was weird he brought his coat when it was warm out (I found out afterward he had used it to hide the ring box). We walked along the Terrace of Infinity and then he led me to an ornate gazebo a few yards away. It was here he got down on one knee and asked me to marry him. He said he could think of no better place than the Terrace of Infinity to make me a promise to love me forever. I said yes through happy tears. Finally, I felt like I belonged.

Adam had grown up in New Hampshire and his parents still lived there. He wanted to settle down and start a family in the Granite State, so in the fall of 2008, I moved in with his folks until he could join us a few months later. I had gotten a job at an organic yogurt company based in the area and loved it. The founder and CEO of the company took a shine to me. He requested I become his special projects manager, helping with speech writing and event planning. The future seemed bright.

Exactly two years after our first date, we got married on Lake Winnipesaukee in front of hundreds of our family and friends. The week leading up to the wedding was stressful, not just because of the planning process, but because my grandmother passed away that Wednesday. She had been in hospice, but it still came as a surprise.

So, on the big day, I felt so many different emotions. Sadness from my grandmother's recent death. Overwhelmed from seeing all my family together in one room. Discomfort from having all eyes on me.

I was overcome with so many feelings and although I didn't specifically ask him for it, I wanted Adam to ask me how I was doing. I needed him to ask how he could support me and show interest in navigating this day together. But it never happened.

As we waited behind the closed doors, getting ready to make our first entrance into the reception as a married couple, I asked him what his favorite part of the day had been. I was still waiting for him to tell me how beautiful I looked, how happy he was to be my husband, or how magical the day had been.

"I like your lip gloss," he said matter-of-factly. This was the only compliment I received from my new husband on our wedding day.

We didn't take a honeymoon right away, but instead waited a few weeks to embark on an Alaskan cruise. I had wanted to go somewhere warm and tropical, but Adam had traveled nearly everywhere in the world except for Alaska. He desperately wanted to go. My people-pleasing tendencies wanted this to be *his* dream vacation, so we bundled up and traveled to see the glaciers.

I wish I could say it was incredibly romantic and we gazed lovingly into each other's eyes every night. I wish I could say we made love all day and expressed our undying devotion for one another. I wish I could say it was everything I'd always imagined my honeymoon would be.

But when I revisit old journal entries from that trip, we were already fighting. A lot.

We returned from our honeymoon and started trying for a baby right away. In my mind, the reason for this was twofold. First, I wasn't getting any younger. I was now thirty-two and my biological clock was ticking. Second, it was also becoming apparent we didn't have a lot in common. Maybe a baby would bring us closer together. Yep—I just cringed reading that, too.

I stopped taking my birth control and we conceived right away. We framed a photo of the positive pregnancy test and gave it to Adam's parents one night at dinner. I was thrilled and we all celebrated. That night, I wrote a journal entry to the baby. I told him or her how excited I was to be their mama and how much I loved them already. The next day, I started bleeding. Two days later, the test was no longer positive. A chemical pregnancy is what the nurse called it, where the egg is fertilized but never implants.

According to an article in *Parents* magazine, "Chemical pregnancy is an early miscarriage that happens within five weeks of implantation... Doctors don't know what causes chemical pregnancy, but it's thought to stem from chromosomal abnormalities that lead to improper development of the embryo." (*Parents*, 2018)

I felt so conflicted. I mourned the baby I wrote to, the one I thought was forming inside of me. And then instantly, I'd feel stupid and ashamed because that hadn't been the case at all. I cried and admonished myself repeatedly over the next several days. I promised myself I wouldn't get excited again until I saw proof in an ultrasound.

So, in early February the following year, when I saw the blinking heart of my baby on the screen, I instantly fell in love.

BIRTHS

In the beginning, I loved being pregnant. My belly grew and I began to feel my baby moving. The first little butterfly flutters turned into full-on somersaults.

I was due in late August, and by early May, I was already huge. I remember going to a baseball game with some friends for my birthday. It was one of the first warm spring days in New Hampshire. I ordered an O'Douls nonalcoholic beer just so I could enjoy a cold beer on a sunny day at a baseball game. But the park didn't allow customers to carry glass bottles, so they poured all beers, non-alcoholic or not, into the same clear plastic cups.

As I waddled to my seat, belly in full view and impossible to miss, I started getting strange looks. I sat down and took a long refreshing swig of my beer. People were definitely staring. That's when I realized they thought I was a very pregnant woman drinking a very alcoholic beer. I wished the bartender could have written "BOOZE-FREE" in Sharpie on my cup. While I tried to enjoy the rest of my beverage, I couldn't help feeling dozens of judging eyes on me. It was my first experience with mom guilt even though I had done nothing wrong. Little did I know, it was just par for the course. Being a mom seems to invite judging eyes and unwarranted advice from strangers constantly.

If I thought I was big in May, I was massive come August. I could no longer see my feet. My ankles were now the same width as my thighs. I simply didn't understand how the skin on my stomach could stretch so much without snapping, like a rubber band pulled too tight. I was finally diagnosed with pre-eclampsia, so they scheduled an induction for the following day.

I won't go into the details of my birth story, but overall, I consider myself lucky. I was in labor for nine hours total and, at 2:34 p.m., gave birth to James, the perfect baby boy. His gender was a surprise to us and the look of pride on Adam's face at having a son was incredibly moving. I was just head over heels with this squishy ball of love and his fuzzy duckling hair.

We were in the hospital for two days and then they let us go home—*with a baby*. I still couldn't believe we could just take this tiny human with us. Some secret part of me kept waiting for his mother to come pick him up.

That's not to say we didn't bond. On the contrary, two days in and I was already a mama bear who would have thrown herself in front of a speeding train for him. But a woman who has just given birth has a lot of confusing and conflicting emotions. One reason is because the lack of sleep makes you an actual crazy person. I was convinced my breast pump was talking to me in those dark early hours of the morning.

But another very common cause for these irrational (and sometimes scary) thoughts is postpartum depression.

One study shows about one in seven new moms suffer from postpartum depression (*CBS News*, 2013). It's a sadness that sets in and just gets heavier and heavier each day. After giving birth, hormones like estrogen and progesterone plummet, which can leave a new mom feeling like nothing will ever feel "normal" again.

In my case, I would sit on the couch and cry for no apparent reason. I loved my baby completely, but when people told me this should be the happiest time in my life, I just cried harder. I'd cry because Adam had to go back to work and I was terrified to be on my own with a week-old baby. I'd cry because when I took a shower, every part of my body was leaking—blood, milk, tears. I felt so alone.

I also had trouble nursing and it was causing me so much stress. "Breast is best!" the lactation consultant from the hospital kept telling me. But I couldn't get James to latch on. I felt like a failure. I couldn't do one of the things my body was created to do. The lactation consultant said to keep trying. I pumped and fed him what little breastmilk I could generate, but my baby was still hungry.

He would scream endlessly, and when one day he barely peed, I realized he was dehydrated. So, I made him a bottle of formula. He gulped it down and finally slept for three hours straight. I was mentally, emotionally, and physically exhausted. When I finally got my doctor on the phone and shared what was going on, she immediately validated my efforts and clarified "*Fed* is best." She also refilled my Zoloft prescription (I had gone off my antidepressants while pregnant) and encouraged me to call anytime.

Within two weeks of me going back on my meds and James feeling full, my world started to brighten again. The darkness once again lifted and I could see through the fog those first several weeks had left behind. Adam and I started a new routine. When he would get home from work, we'd have dinner together and then I would go into the guest room. I would try to be asleep by 6:00 p.m. so when Adam brought the monitor in at midnight, I would have had at least six straight hours. Sometimes James wouldn't wake up until 2:00 a.m., which gave me *eight* full hours of sleep. To a new mom, this is better than winning a million dollars and having it hand delivered by Ryan Gosling. Okay, maybe it's equal.

The rest of my maternity leave flew by and I was back at work just after Thanksgiving. When I was on maternity leave, the founder and CEO of the yogurt company I worked for granted my long-awaited move to the public relations team. I would now be managing all social media and blogger outreach for their baby brand. It was the perfect fit.

Those early years of motherhood seem like a blur in my mind. Adam and I had some fun adventures with James. We went on a Caribbean cruise. We went down to Florida to see my mom. We took weekend trips to Maine and Boston.

On one such Boston excursion, we'd gone to the aquarium, and on a walk afterward, we stopped to watch a group of break-dancers. About seven young men were spinning and sliding in ways that made their bodies appear to be boneless. All three of us were in awe, but especially eighteen-month-old James. He couldn't take his eyes off the street acrobatics.

When we got home, we noticed he kept attempting this move where he would plant both hands on the ground and kick and twist his leg outwards. We'd never seen him do this before, and it reminded me of something I'd seen before.

"Oh my God, he's mimicking the break-dancers!" I gasped when I remembered where I'd witnessed those moves.

"He totally is!" agreed Adam.

So, we did the only thing two young parents in 2012 would do. We pulled out the camcorder and uploaded the video to YouTube. With the soundtrack of Young M.C.'s *Bust a Move*, obviously.

It's still on there today. I recently showed it to nearly eleven-year-old James, and he eyed it with an expression I know so well. There was a mix of wonder and embarrassment and a little pride he had a dance video online, pre-TikTok.

It would be another year or so before we'd start thinking about giving James a sibling. But in the meantime, something horrific happened—an event that changed the course of so many lives. A terrible incident nobody saw coming.

PART TWO:

THE RECALCULATING

"Start now. Start where you are. Start with fear. Start with pain. Start with doubt. Start with hands shaking. Start with voice trembling but start. Start and don't stop. Start where you are, with what you have. Just...start."

—IJEOMA UMEBINYUO

CHAPTER 5

Life is full of ebbs and flows. This is the yin and yang of the human experience. There is no good without the bad. There is no light without shadows. It is the juxtaposition that allows celebrations to be sweeter because we know of tragedies—the proof we lived through them and came out on the other side.

The first quarter of my life was full of such dichotomies. In childhood, I experienced abandonment as well as unconditional love. In adolescence, through loss, I found belonging. In college, I perfected how to hide, but also how to shine. And in adulthood, I had finally created the life I'd always wanted. Or so I thought.

***

INTRODUCTIONS

I was twenty-six when my dad told me he was getting a divorce from Demi. I felt a sense of relief as twenty years of walking on eggshells would now be over. He even admitted one of the reasons he was leaving was because of how she'd treated me as a child. My sense of justice was short-lived, though, because in the same breath, he told me he'd met someone else. Her name was Beth and he'd met her at the gym. I was skeptical.

She was twenty years younger than him and because I vowed to be honest in this book, I'll share my true first impression. I thought she was with him for his money. Maybe it's all the *Dateline* episodes I've seen about younger wives poisoning their older husbands to steal their money. She was tiny, blonde, and athletic, and I just didn't understand why a forty-year-old woman would be interested in a sixty-year-old man.

However, after spending an extended amount of time with them, I witnessed real love. Her bubbly personality brought out a child-like excitement in him I'd never seen before. They traveled and went dancing. For the first time I could remember, I saw my father happy.

So, when he told me they were getting married, I gave him my blessing and support.

Beth had a daughter, Maddie, who was seven years old at the time. Adorable and spunky, the first time I met her, I asked about the pink number seven Pittsburgh Steelers jersey she wore.

"Is the number seven for how old you are?" I inquired innocently. I know nothing about sports.

"Um, no. It's for Ben Roethlisberger, only the best quarterback in the NFL."

I smiled. I loved her fire already.

On the day of the wedding, we all met at the Washington, DC hotel where the intimate ceremony and reception would take place. Beth wore a beautiful black dress with a rhinestone collar. Dad wore a dark tailored suit. They exchanged some brief vows and we sat down for dinner. Guests made toasts and as the wine began to spread warmly in my belly, I clinked my glass. The din of conversation quieted. All eyes turned to me as my breath caught in my chest.

I stood up and looked right at Beth. Then, through welling eyes, I mustered the words, "I've never seen my dad this happy before. Thank you for bringing him back to life."

When I looked at my dad, I saw genuine love and respect for me. I was so hopeful this would be a new chapter in our relationship. Optimistic we'd finally be able to have some honest conversations and mend the enormous rift that had been between us for so long.

Over the next six years, we did just that. Little by little, conversation after conversation, we got closer. And when I brought James into this world, you'd have thought I gave him the best present he never knew he wanted.

My dad loved being a grandfather. He'd come to visit and hold baby James on his chest while he napped. He'd sit and stare at him for hours. I'd marvel at this side of my dad I had never seen. I wasn't ready to forgive him yet but watching him engage and show such unabashed love toward James, I felt some of my old grudges begin to melt away. I felt a newly formed connection to my father.

In 2012, Dad came to our house for Thanksgiving, but he didn't bring Beth or Maddie. I didn't pry and he eventually pulled me aside to share what was going on. She had some mental health challenges she was working through and needed time away from my father. They had decided to separate.

He was distraught and I felt so sad for him. He had moved out and was living in an apartment. He didn't know if they would reconcile. His world seemed to be crumbling and he had very little in the way of a support system. I told him I would help in any way I could.

We kept communication alive over the next few months, and in the spring, Adam and I brought James to visit him in DC. We stayed with some friends the first night, and on the second night, my dad was going to take James on his own so Adam and I could go out in the city where we'd met. We met up for lunch and my dad took James back with him to his apartment. He sent photos from the playground and said they were having a blast.

About halfway through putting on my makeup for our big night out, my dad called, and I could hear James crying in the background.

"He wants his mama," was all I heard, so I changed my plans to stay at Dad's that night and sent Adam out with our friends.

I spent the evening with James and my dad, and he shared some promising news. He told me he and Beth had been talking about a reconciliation. In fact, he went to see her the night before at the house they once shared. He seemed hopeful he would be moving back there soon.

I was so happy for him and it seemed like things were on an upswing. When we woke up Sunday morning, we drove to a restaurant in northern Virginia to have brunch with Adam and his cousin.

The restaurant was buzzing with young people. There was a line at the Bloody Mary bar and Vampire Weekend crooned over the speakers. The smell of bacon wafted from every direction and my brioche French toast and mimosas made for a sweet ending to the weekend. I was content.

But halfway through the meal, my dad got quiet. I noticed him staring out the window, his eyes glazed over while looking at nothing in particular. I asked him what was wrong, and he said he had a weird feeling. He couldn't explain it but remained silent for the remainder of the meal. I continued to glance at him intermittently and made a mental note to bring it up again later.

Flying back home to New Hampshire that afternoon, I thought about his unusual behavior. It happened around 10 a.m.—the time the coroner said Beth died.

GOODBYES

Minutes after finally falling into bed after the long day of traveling, my phone rang. It was my dad, and he was screaming.

Trying to decipher words through his hysteria, I finally understood what he was saying.

"She killed herself."

I had never, and haven't since, heard such pain in someone's voice. It was palpable through the guttural sounds he made and the hopelessness of his moaning. Over and over, he repeated those three words bookmarked only by more screaming.

I began bawling and sunk to the floor. I crawled into my closet and rolled myself into a ball. My bare legs were itchy from the carpet underneath and now wet with my tears. Nausea overwhelmed me. I couldn't stop visualizing the grotesque scene and envisioning my distraught father outside, ambulance lights flashing and police swarming the house.

I didn't say it out loud, but "What's going to happen to Maddie?" was on repeat in my mind. Now fourteen years old, Beth always had full custody because Maddie's dad traveled frequently for work. *Who would look after her now?* My heart cracked completely open for her and my dad in that moment. As I rocked back and forth, I began to formulate a plan. I needed to be there.

"I'll get a flight tomorrow. I love you, Dad. I won't let you go through this alone," I told him. I'm not sure he heard me, or if he did, that my words even registered, but as soon as we hung up, I booked a flight back to DC and started packing.

Adam had poked his head in the closet to see what was going on during all of this. I couldn't get my words out, so instead of coming over to comfort me, he turned around and went back to bed. At the time, it didn't even bother me. It was par for the course in our marriage.

However, thinking about this now, I feel incredibly sad. I assume Adam believed one of two things. Either Chandra is so strong and independent, she doesn't need me. Or this is too much to deal with so I'm going to ignore it. Either way, it's not the reaction I needed or deserved and I still have lingering resentment about it.

I couldn't sleep at all that night. I Googled flights and cried alone in the bathroom.

In the morning I told Adam, "I found a flight and it leaves this morning. You're going to have to take care of James for a few days. I have to be with my dad during this."

"Okay," he responded flatly.

Not unlike my wedding day, I waited for him to ask me how I was feeling. I waited for him to hold me, comfort me, and tell me he was there for me. I waited for him to ask me what he could do.

I'm still waiting.

When I arrived at BWI the next day, my dad was there to pick me up. His ashen face and sunken eyes immediately ignited a fresh onslaught of tears. We didn't speak much on the drive. We didn't speak much for the next couple of days. It was like Dad was in a trance as he made funeral arrangements and dealt with the aftermath of Beth's death.

I was surprised when he told me he often felt her near him. He said he could physically feel the pressure of her body when he felt his lowest and it brought him some sense of comfort. I didn't know what to think, but it felt like he was making his way back into the land of the living, like a baby calf just beginning to lift its head toward the warm sunshine. I was grateful I was able to support him through this time.

On the day of the funeral, when he was in the shower, I spoke out loud to Beth. If she really was around watching over him, I needed to ask her to do something for me.

I whispered into the still air, "Beth? If you're there, I need you to keep watching over my dad until he's okay. It brings him a sense of peace, and he needs that right now, more than anything. I'm angry, Beth. I don't understand why you did it, and I hate seeing him like this. Please, continue to bring him comfort, and send me a sign so I know you hear me."

While I waited for my sign, I looked around at my dad's apartment. He hadn't decorated, as I knew he hoped it was only temporary, but there were framed photos. There were ones of me, Adam, James, Maddie, and one of Dad and Beth on their wedding day. I thought back to the joy we all felt that day and a fresh wave of sadness washed over me.

It was at that moment I heard my sign.

It came in the sound I can only describe as a piece of metal dropping into the pipes above my head. A clattering noise began directly over my head, ran across the ceiling to the window, and then stopped abruptly. It lasted about ten seconds in total, and to this day, there is no practical explanation for the noise. My dad said he'd never heard anything like what I described.

It was then I knew he had been telling the truth. Beth was here and she was going to stay with him for as long as he needed. She would not be heading into the white light until *he* was ready.

At the funeral home, we gathered in folding chairs in a small room. The overwhelming attendance left many standing, but I was able to grab a chair toward the back, allowing my dad, Maddie, her dad, and other such immediate family members to sit in the front row. Then, Maddie went up to the closed casket, got out her guitar, and played a song she had written that week for her mother.

She sang, "Seven days since you've been here, reminiscing on these fourteen years, all I knew was you and me. And suddenly, you had to leave."

There wasn't one person in the room who wasn't crying hysterically.

We wept for the little girl whose mother left too soon. We sobbed for the future milestones she'd cross and the life she'd lead, all without the woman who had raised her.

We also wept for the woman who had taken her own life. For what it must have felt like to be in such a dark place. To believe you have no other options. To be so done with this world you leave it willingly. Imagining that frame of mind can stir something dark within us, something we don't want to examine because we begin to ask, *what if?*

What if I had been there?

What if things had been different?

What if it had been me?

Later in the day, it was time for me to head back to New Hampshire, to my husband and son, to my job, and to my "normal" life. I don't know if I realized it at the time, but something had shifted between my father and me. An invisible wall had crumbled and we finally saw each other as flawed and grieving humans desperate for connection. The tides turned that day in my relationship with my dad.

The wound his abandonment had left finally stopped bleeding. It would still take years to begin the healing process, but *his* role in the battle of *my* self-worth was over. He had surrendered and a slight sense of peace washed over me even amidst the bloody aftermath of a decades-long war. The void that had existed for over thirty years was finally starting to fill with my father's love.

TISSUES

In the days and weeks after Beth's death, life was bleak. Colors seemed dulled. Smiles were harder to come by. I began questioning what life even meant anymore and watching my dad enter a severe depression was harder to witness than I ever could have imagined.

One night while on the phone, he told me he had his own thoughts of suicide. Dad said he knew exactly how he'd do it because he'd done his research. This bombshell shocked me to my core. I sat with the information and contemplated how it would have felt if he'd gone through with it. The abandonment wound I carried was still tender. If he left me again, I don't know if it ever would have fully healed. I certainly wouldn't be the person I am today.

Ultimately, he decided not to do it and he confessed the main reason was me. He knew how devastated I would be and how it would destroy me in unimaginable ways. He was right and I thanked him not only for sharing this with me, but for choosing life.

Conversations like this became more natural and more frequent. He continued to share stories of experiencing Beth's spirit. She came to him often in those early days. He'd feel the weight of her when he couldn't sleep. A framed photo of the two of them inexplicably fell from a shelf one day. He knew she was always near and it soothed his pain a little.

I worried about him constantly, but also about Maddie. She was only fourteen and had just lost her mother. My dad was in no state to take care of a teenage girl and her own father was always out of town. Adam and I talked about what was best for her and decided she should come live with us. I approached my dad with the idea, and although he shared his appreciation for the gesture, he had been thinking of an alternative solution.

Nashville.

Since she was eight, Maddie practiced the guitar every day and had become a proficient singer and songwriter. In the year before Beth's death, Maddie had been playing gigs around the Montgomery County circuit in Maryland. Some shows took place at coffee shops and some even at bars. She had been playing and singing covers, as well as some of her original songs. Moving to Nashville to become a country singer had always been one of her dreams.

My dad grew up in Memphis and still had a twinge of a southern accent, even after living in the Northeast for decades. He didn't want to live in his apartment anymore but couldn't bear the thought of living in the house where Beth took her life. So, he talked to Maddie's father (the two of them had bonded over this whole experience and had become close) and requested to move her to Tennessee.

Maddie's dad agreed, and my dad sold the Maryland house. He took the money and purchased a huge five-bedroom home in Hendersonville, about twenty minutes outside Nashville. Taylor Swift had once lived in the same town, so Maddie was enamored. My kids still call this house "Granddad's Mansion."

The other wonderful part of living in Nashville was the family they'd have nearby. My aunt and uncle lived a couple hours away in Mississippi, and their daughters both lived in Nashville proper. My dad purchased the house in November of 2014 and allowed one of my cousins, a twenty-four-year-old teacher, to move in and "keep it warm" so she could save on rent.

My dad retired from his job as president of a large architecture firm a few months later and he and Maddie officially moved down south in the summer of 2015. She started her sophomore year of high school that fall, and they both seemed almost happy again.

Over these two years, my dad and I consistently got closer. We began having real honest conversations. I learned about his youth and the issues he had with my grandparents. He told me about how he met my mom and then left shortly thereafter to fight in Vietnam. I asked questions about the early years he lived with us.

We talked about how I felt when he was married to Demi and he apologized. He finally took responsibility for his role in the manipulation and shared how he felt he needed to choose a side. He had already blown up his first marriage and couldn't do it again. And when my brother was born, he made a promise to himself to stick it out.

I confided I had always felt his love was conditional on my behavior and he acknowledged how I might feel that way. Then he recounted a memory that catalyzed an important shift in my perspective.

He reminded me of how I would cry on the way home from my weekends with him. As confused as I was about his feelings for me, I loved him immensely. And I missed him. Even when I was with him, I missed him.

So, every other Sunday night on the trip back to Mom's, my crying would commence, and he would drive silently, looking only at the road in front of him. I would bunch up my tissues and leave them in the handle of the passenger door. I would enter my mom's house with my heart and stomach tied together in knots. I didn't know if my longing was reciprocated. I didn't know if my father missed me as much as I missed him.

The story he divulged next was one I had never even imagined.

Unbeknownst to me, once I entered my mom's house, he would sit in his tan Volvo, reach over to grab my damp tissues, and inhale the scent of his daughter's tears. This would unleash his own and leave him sobbing in his car, sometimes for hours.

Envisioning this scene, now as a parent myself, gutted me. It occurred to me that maybe, just maybe, he hadn't built his walls because he *didn't* love me. Instead, maybe he built them to protect his own heart because he loved me *so much*.

I shared this reflection with him one day and it was like I had unlocked some piece of him. His tears flowed freely, and he confirmed this is what he felt he had to do to survive being away from me and only seeing me two weekends a month. He had to keep me at a distance, so he didn't fall apart.

Even writing this now, my eyes tear up. This was a profound discovery that initiated a wave of forgiveness—forgiveness for my father's actions, yes, but also forgiveness for myself. The feelings I had growing up were validated and I finally understood them in a way I couldn't have at such a young age. This single conversation began to unravel something in me and started an evolution that would change the course of my life.

CHAPTER 6

The realization of my father's love for me was life-changing.

It was as if a wound opened when he left so many years before. I spent decades unsuccessfully trying to fill it with boys and booze and people-pleasing behaviors. Adam became a Band-Aid for a while, but reconciling with my dad was the first time it truly had a chance to start healing.

The visceral need for validation and unconditional love from my husband I'd felt in the beginning became less intense. As the wound began to heal, so did my sense of self.

***

PRAYERS

Even though our marriage wasn't on steady ground, Adam and I had been trying for another baby. You may be thinking, *why on earth would you do that*? The truth is it just felt like our family wasn't complete yet. Some part of me knew we were meant to have a second child together.

We'd started a few months before Beth's death but weren't having any luck. Finally, after eight months of temperature-taking and tracking, I called an infertility doctor. They usually want a patient to have been trying for at least a year, but I was thirty-five and of "advanced maternal age," so they let me make an appointment. (Side note: As bad as the term "advanced maternal age" sounds, it's still better than "geriatric pregnancy," another phrase I'd heard.) The kind doctor was of his own advanced age and agreed to write me a prescription for Clomid, a medication to help with infertility.

After the first cycle, I got my positive pregnancy test. Since I had experienced loss before, I tempered my excitement and was anxious to attend the first ultrasound to see the heartbeat for myself. Finally, at eight weeks pregnant, there it was—a blinking light on the screen that gave me such incredible hope.

And then Adam said, "Wait. What's that?"

A second blinking. A second heartbeat. Twins.

We knew this was a possibility due to the fertility drugs but were astounded just the same. We walked around the rest of the day in a daze. We felt excitement for the new lives growing inside me and fear of how to manage twins. Over the next four weeks, I researched every thought passing through my mind. Most seemed like a logistical nightmare.

My Google searches included: "How do you nurse two babies?" "How do you carry two babies?" "When one baby is in the crib, and one is out, where do you put the one that's out to pick up the one that's still inside? On the floor?"

I still don't have an answer for that last one.

Gathering information is how I settle my nerves, and I must admit, it was working. I began envisioning two identical cherubic faces staring up at me, smiling and cooing. I could see two little ones wearing matching outfits on their first day of preschool. I read about the special bond of twins and felt lucky to bring two more miracles into the world.

I brought a list of questions to ask the doctor when we went in for our twelve-week ultrasound. Laying back on the crinkly paper of the exam table, I had finally gotten my head around everything and was excited to see those two little blinking hearts.

When the nurse turned the screen toward us, we saw the first one. Flickering steadily, that light became my north star. We'd made it into the second trimester. Hallelujah!

But as the nurse moved the cold gel around my belly, she got quiet. We didn't see a second blinking.

"I'm just going to get the doctor. I'll be right back," she said and then left the room.

There was only silence as my head began to spin with worst-case scenarios. Adam and I didn't speak. It was not until I heard the words from the doctor's mouth that I allowed the tears to fall.

"I'm so sorry, but it looks like the other baby is gone."

It's so hard to lose something you never knew you wanted and then realized you did.

"The baby you still have is looking great, though. We'll see you back here in four weeks."

Both a consolation and a congratulations—you still get one healthy baby, so be happy! I don't think I ever fully allowed myself to grieve the baby I lost. I, and seemingly everyone around me, just wanted to move on.

We learned later what had happened was called Vanishing Twin Syndrome.

"Vanishing Twin Syndrome occurs when twins are seen on an early ultrasound, but one of the gestational sacs or fetuses has 'disappeared' on a later ultrasound," says Dr. Mark Payson, a reproductive endocrinologist who also serves as the medical director of CCRM Northern Virginia, an infertility clinic (*Parents*, 2017).

"The vanishing twin generally stops developing and is absorbed back into the uterus, which accounts for its apparent disappearance," according to Dr. Payson. He estimates that around 20 percent of twin pregnancies end this way (*Parents*, 2017).

In writing this book, I've often thought of my baby who "vanished." By telling this story, I hope to honor him or her with love and grace, believing we'll be reunited someday.

We found out the gender this time and were excited to give James a little brother. We agreed on the name Jack to keep the "J" names going strong. I had invited my mom to stay for a month after Jack was born, both to help me out and mitigate any postpartum depression this time around. Everything was going well.

Then, at thirty-six weeks, I was getting a pedicure with a friend in anticipation of the upcoming big day. Sitting in the plastic chair of the nail salon, waiting for our toes to dry, I felt something wet in my seat.

"Oh my God, I think my water just broke!" I exclaimed and proceeded to wipe my hand under myself to see what was happening.

Fresh, red blood covered my hand.

With terror in my eyes, I showed my friend my bloody hand, and she calmly said, "Okay. I'm calling 911. Don't move."

I couldn't move. I couldn't breathe. I could not lose Jack.

This was when I had my first experience with my inner knowing. A voice somewhere deep inside of me provided clear instructions: Whatever happened, I was *not to stand up*. I held onto this order from some unseen source, and it became like a mantra for me to repeat instead of going into shock.

Don't stand up. Don't stand up. Don't stand up.

The ambulance came, and two EMTs brought a gurney into the nail salon. I told them I wasn't able to stand, so they lifted me in a sitting position onto the thin mattress. There I sat, repeating my mantra, until I got ahold of Adam to ensure he was on his way.

When we got to the hospital, they rolled me into the emergency room. When the nurse came in, I told her I felt like I needed to pee but was afraid to stand up. She said it was okay, she was there, and the inner voice agreed. So, I stood up, made it three steps to the toilet, and then blood began gushing from my body.

My knees weakened, and the nurse led me to the toilet. Huge clots of blood fell out of me, and I began to pass out. She used smelling salts and persuaded me to stay with her. They got me back onto the gurney and hooked me up to check my baby's vitals.

Jack wasn't moving.

They rushed me to surgery and performed an emergency C-section. It was taking too long for the epidural to work, so I told them just to knock me out. Then blackness.

When I woke up, my throat was scratchy, and I was disoriented. I didn't hear any crying, and a visceral fear took over. The entire lower part of my body was numb, and it felt like my brain was ten steps behind. It was trying to catch up to the terror my body was experiencing. I looked around and saw a hospital room, heard the monitors' beeping, but still no baby. I finally saw Adam, but I couldn't speak because the nurse had just removed the intubation tube. He jumped up and recognized the panic in my eyes.

"Jack is in the NICU. They're helping him breathe and the next twenty-four hours are critical," Adam said, almost robotically. His engineer brain was looking for scientific facts and solutions. It was how he dealt with his fear of the unknown. I closed my eyes and began to pray.

It wasn't the kind of praying I had done as a child, on my knees at the end of the bed, talking out loud to God and asking for things. It was a new kind of praying, a full-body praying that enveloped me and blasted out love. An energetic firework display, sending out pieces of my soul to my little boy, teetering on the edge of life and death.

I don't know how long I did this for, as I was in and out of consciousness. The doctors had me on pain meds for my C-section, and for what felt like my breaking heart. I didn't end up needing a blood transfusion but came close. I couldn't walk, so at some point that evening, they wheeled my bed up to the NICU so I could see Jack.

He was laying in his incubator, tubes spiraling out of his nose and stomach. Monitors were beeping, and there was a cloth over his eyes, I assume to offer him a sense of darkness. My tears flowed, and I began to pray again. I willed every cell in my body to send him healing energy. All my love. All my light.

The next morning, I was able to get into a wheelchair, so Adam and I joined the NICU doctor on his rounds. There was nothing new to report, but I could sit next to Jack and continue this new kind of praying that was starting to feel like second nature to me. Washing the purest love over him, directly from my heart, soul, and mind, was the only thing I knew to do.

That afternoon, nearly twenty-four hours after sitting in the nail salon, Jack began to breathe on his own.

His recovery afterward was nothing short of miraculous. We were allowed to go home within five days because he was back up to his birth weight. He had trouble nursing, but took to the bottle right away, so I pumped day and night, trying to match the determination of my newborn son, who had beat all odds of survival.

I later found out I'd had a placental abruption—a condition where the placenta (the pouch that holds and feeds the fetus) had detached too early. As a result, Jack was not getting enough of the oxygen or nutrients he needed to survive.

According to the March of Dimes, this happens to one in one hundred women with varying levels of severity (March of Dimes, 2021). In my case, it was severe enough that it was life-threatening to both of us and could have had such a different outcome.

If I hadn't been at that particular nail salon, I wouldn't have been just a couple of miles from the only local hospital with a NICU. If I had stood up at any point before my inner voice told me it was okay, neither of us would likely be here today. I had planned on going to Target after the nail salon. What if this had all happened an hour later?

I might not be here to write this book.

This entire experience was such a wake-up call in so many ways. The fragility of life. The power of prayer. Faith in a higher power. Something bigger than us was looking over Jack and me that day and was communicating with me directly through my inner knowing. This was the first spark of my spiritual awakening.

I look at Jack now, seven years old and happy. So solid and sturdy, funny and kind, he is a miracle. Every night for the past seven years, I've prayed a full-body prayer of love and light for him and his brother, sending pieces of my soul to them while they sleep.

DOSES

I was so relieved to have my mom stay with us for the first six weeks Jack was home. Not only had I been worried about experiencing postpartum depression again, but I also wasn't sure how to parent two children. James was only three at the time and still needed lots of attention, so having my mom there to support me was a lifesaver.

Each day I sent up a little prayer of gratitude that Jack and I had made it through such a terrifying experience. I felt like he and I were saved for a reason. Like there were so many things we both had left to do on this earth. The feeling was immense but peaceful at the same time. My inner knowing and I were becoming fast friends.

I didn't share any of this with Adam because I didn't think he'd understand. I figured he'd just make fun of it, and I didn't want my newfound beliefs in something greater to be minimized. He also started going out. A lot. Friday nights with the boys became a regular thing, along with some Saturdays. When my mom brought up her observations of his absence one night over dinner, I defended him.

"Mom, he's busy at work and needs time to decompress," I said half-heartedly as she rolled her eyes and gave up.

What hits me now, writing this story, is the fact that this was his reaction to very nearly losing his wife and newborn son. Instead of increasing his time with us, he did the opposite. Maybe that was how he dealt with the trauma of what had just happened. Maybe he was using alcohol to hide from his big feelings. I certainly knew that game well.

But in his hiding, I felt abandoned. I felt like he dosed out his love and affection when it suited his needs, never mine. So, in moments of loneliness, I tried to make those love doses last. I'd remind myself of all the reasons I still loved him and the good times we'd had together.

Over the following months, the doses became increasingly rare. Adam traveled during the week for work and then was out with friends nearly every weekend. So, on the occasions when we were together, and I felt like I could, I brought it up.

I told him I felt like the kids and I were not at the top of his priority list, and I was incredibly lonely.

Sometimes he'd apologize and offer me a love dose. But, many times, he would deny it. His best defense was always an offense, so the conversation would turn into an argument about who did more for our family. Once, he even recommended we list all the things we each do throughout the day and compare. In instances like this, I usually ended up sighing and walking away.

Many times, I brought up the idea of marriage counseling. I'd had so much luck with Lisa all those years back and several other positive therapy experiences since then.

"We're both so frustrated. I think it could help us to hear each other better. Maybe give us some new techniques to try," I suggested one night when he wasn't traveling.

He had denied my request so many times, so I expected a similar reaction. I was pleasantly surprised when instead he answered, "Fine. I'll go to a session."

I booked an appointment with a local marriage counselor, and we showed up, awkward and nervous. Sitting on another worn green couch, I shared the things troubling me in our marriage.

The thing you have to understand about Adam is he can be incredibly charming. He can turn it on and off on a whim. And when we sat in our sixty-minute therapy session, he had it turned way up. He said all the right things and imitated empathy for my struggles. We held hands, and I felt closer to him than I had in years. But the moment we left and got back into the car, he looked over at me and said, "Well, that was a waste of an hour."

We never went back to counseling, and my feelings of loneliness and resentment continued to grow.

PATHS

All of my days began to blend together. I would wake up, get the boys ready, and drop them off at school and daycare. I'd then commute an hour to my job, sit in my cubicle answering emails and putting out fires for eight hours, and drive the hour home. Finally, if I made it back in time to see them, I'd get the boys ready for bed. Once they were down, I'd open my bottle of wine and zone out in front of the TV.

At that time in our lives, Adam and I generally stayed out of each other's way. We were both so stressed by the end of the day, it was best to give one another space. Sometimes when he drank, he would say incredibly hurtful things—about me, my family, anything he could to hit his target, which was inevitably my self-worth. Sometimes he would glare at me with a look I interpreted as pure hatred. Unfortunately, the feeling was becoming mutual.

We hid our struggles well, which was easy because he was traveling so often for work. When he wasn't traveling, he was often out with his buddies. We had reached a point where we didn't even enjoy spending time together. It usually ended up in an argument or hurt feelings, and the drinking always made it worse.

I would rationalize it to myself. I'd write in my journal, "No marriage is perfect. He doesn't really mean the things he says. I'm just too sensitive. Maybe if I hadn't taken offense to that comment, things wouldn't have blown up like they did. I just need to try harder. I'm just as much at fault in this, maybe even more."

This is how I thought life was supposed to be.

Some of these ongoing dialogues were only internal, but some were actual commentary from previous arguments. At the time, I had never heard the word *gaslighting*, but looking back, it's what our relationship had become. A series of hurtful comments later covered up with shame for not being able to "take a joke."

Psychologists use the term "gaslighting" to refer to a specific type of manipulation that tries to get someone else (or a group of people) to question their own reality, memory, or perceptions (NBC News, 2018).

According to Robin Stern, PhD, Associate Director of the Yale Center for Emotional Intelligence and author of *The Gaslight Effect*, "It may start out with seemingly small offenses. But the problem is that even more-or-less insignificant instances of you questioning your own judgment or reality—thanks to the deliberate intent of someone else—can snowball. You can end up in a cycle of not being able to negotiate your daily life in a way where you are clear-minded, can focus, can make sound decisions, and have a sense of well-being." (NBC News, 2018)

This is how I felt, and I thought I was to blame. I didn't stand up for myself. I allowed my self-worth to be determined by someone else, and instead of being brave, I hid. I kept it all in and washed it down each day with red wine and rolling eyes. I was so judgmental of people who appeared to have it all together. Everyone else seemed to have a loving, supportive partner, immaculate children who were exceeding every developmental milestone, a bustling social life, and world travel.

The funny thing is, I'm sure when people looked at *my* social media, that's exactly what they saw too. We highlight and edit to make our lives shinier to the outside world. It becomes almost a contest to prove who has the most perfect kids, the most perfect home, the most perfect partner, the most perfect life. When, in reality, so many of us are behind the cameras with unbrushed hair, swollen eyes, and a heavy heart.

Wouldn't it be amazing if we could all just bare those parts of ourselves so others wouldn't feel so alone? But no one on Facebook wants to see how sad we are. Nobody wants to see the cracks because then they'd have to face their own.

Nope, shiny and edited is the way we go. So, I kept pushing it down and assuming this was just how life was going to be for me. This was the life I had signed up for, and this was what I had to look forward to for the next several decades—feeling unseen, unheard, unknown.

Then one night, while I was lying in bed and scrolling through Facebook, I saw a post from a high school friend. She had recently announced she was getting divorced and shared photos of the new apartment she'd rented for herself and her two boys. I'm sure some people saw the post and liked it out of pity, sad that one of us was divorcing and hoping to God it wouldn't be them next.

But not for me. That post sparked something in me I hadn't felt in years. *Hope.*

I sat up in bed, scouring her Facebook post intently. I realized I was *jealous* of her, of her new apartment and independence. Although this realization shouldn't have shocked me, it honestly did. I had never allowed myself to imagine what it would be like to leave my marriage.

After seeing the Facebook post, I started having dreams about being on my own. About having my own place for the boys and me and living life in whichever way I wanted. I dreamed about feeling safe and secure in my own skin.

It was also around this time I began hearing James Bay's *Let It Go* everywhere I went. I can't legally share the lyrics here, but Google them—it felt like a message just for me.

It was like I was on this one path, the one society expected of me. It was straight and shiny but brought me dread and sadness. And then, out of the corner of my eye, this Facebook post illuminated an alternate path. I couldn't see where it led, but it felt *right* somehow. Everything inside me wanted to sneak over to that other path just to soak in its sunlight and breathe in its sweet smell of freedom.

CHAPTER 7

When you hear the term "midlife crisis," what scenario springs to mind?

Perhaps it's one of balding men buying shiny red sports cars and having affairs with much younger women? Or maybe it's one of beer-bellied dads trying to squeeze themselves into their high school jerseys, pining for the "good old days"? Whatever the imagined image, for me, it always reeked of unrealized dreams and heavy regret.

I had always assumed that first, only men had them, and second, they always involved some sort of regression. A ferocious grasping at youth while it poured like sand through their fingers. I only knew what I had seen in movies or read in books, so I wholly looked down my nose at the mere concept of a midlife crisis.

Until I had my own.

***

RENEWALS

I had glimpsed another path and now, I couldn't unsee it. I constantly pondered the ways I could make my way over to it. At the time, I didn't realize I was having a midlife crisis because none of the scenarios mentioned above applied to me. First, I was a woman, and as far as I knew, women didn't have midlife crises. And second, I wasn't feeling any sense of going backward—day and night, I was focused on the possibilities of my future.

I recently listened to a podcast featuring Stacy London, an American stylist and author known best as co-host on TLC's *What Not to Wear*. London was a guest on the *Everything is Fine* podcast, and she voiced a term I enthusiastically memorized: *midlife renaissance*.

"I'm a little tired of the whole idea of a midlife crisis...I am much more interested in having a midlife renaissance. But I kind of feel like you don't get to one without the other," said London. "And if we're all going to live to be, you know, in our nineties or hundreds, we have a lot more time on the planet being old than young. And it's what we're doing with the middle, what we're doing with these pivots, with these crises, in a way that allows us to evolve as modern women." (*Everything is Fine*, 2020)

Preach, sister.

I do believe for women, a midlife crisis is much different. It's less cringy, more empowering. A re-awakening. A renewal. A *renaissance*.

The concept of a midlife renaissance isn't new. Self-help literature has been around for over a hundred years (*Time*, 2016). People have always embraced a quest for knowledge and personal development. An interest in the evolution of the human psyche.

My midlife renaissance didn't just happen one day out of the blue. It started as a whisper but graduated quickly into an incessant nagging. Pretty soon, it was a deafening insistence that things were just not right. It became impossible to ignore.

I looked in the mirror and despised the person staring back at me. Who was this woman who said yes to everyone except herself? Who was this woman who couldn't finish anything she started? Who was this woman who judged everyone around her but refused to take off the rose-colored glasses when it came to her own life?

I certainly didn't recognize her, nor did I want anything to do with her. She was cranky and cynical and incredibly sad. It was as if her life no longer fit. Like too-tight jeans, trying to squeeze herself into a pair that looked great on the rack, but she couldn't breathe.

I wish I could say I just woke up one day, knew what I needed to do, and started taking action. But the truth is, I didn't do anything. For years, I clung to those too-tight jeans and refused to take them off. They were *the* jeans, the ones that used to fit perfectly, the ones that once gave me so much self-confidence. If I took them off and faced the fact that they no longer fit, where would that leave me?

Naked and alone, I feared.

A book I picked up one day loosened the top button, and for the first time in so long, I felt a tiny bit of relief. It was called *Rising Strong* by Brené Brown, and in it, she talked about how vulnerability was a strength. Being vulnerable with another human was the bravest thing you could do because as Queen Brené said, "We are hardwired to connect with others; it's what gives purpose and meaning to our lives, and without it there is suffering." (Brown, 2015).

I was suffering because I wasn't connecting. Not with others, and certainly not with myself. I was too busy trying not to get hurt. The walls I started building the night of the crickets now fully enveloped me. Nobody was able to get in.

But I knew that if I wanted to breathe again, I needed to break down those walls. I needed to rip off those jeans.

I began to practice vulnerability like one might practice the piano—tentatively at first, but eventually with a flourish. The act of opening up to others about how I was feeling, really feeling, created a salve that soothed the rawness of my pain. I began to see how others were also feeling lost and unseen. That they too had a sense of things being "off." I wasn't alone in my crisis any longer. I allowed myself to be naked, to be vulnerable. I was entering a full-blown renaissance.

By definition, a renaissance is "a renewed interest in something." (Oxford Languages, 2021)

Yes, that was it! I had found a renewed interest in life. In actually *living* it, not just going through the motions. Not just doing the things I was told I *should* be doing; I had a renewed interest in figuring out who I was and what I wanted.

I began to see the debris blocking my path for what it really was.

That pile of branches over there? That's from the time my dad shooed me away, teaching me my needs don't matter.

That big rock? Oh, that's from when Katie didn't want to be my friend, confirming I'm unlovable.

That pile of dirt? That's from the night in St. John when I learned people take what they want and don't care if it breaks you.

All of that shit blocking my path? Each item was a belief I had developed about myself over the years. Each belief, a lie I would eventually unlearn.

BREAKDOWNS

Like the inner voice I heard when I went into labor with Jack, I felt so strongly I was meant to follow this alternate path. I just *knew* it was for me. My high school friend's Facebook post had shifted something deep inside me, and I finally admitted to myself that Adam and I were not meant to be together forever. Some piece of me knew divorce was inevitable, but instead of dread, a sense of peace washed over me.

Every time I would attempt to continue down the original path, the voice of my soul would repeat "recalculating" incessantly, like the annoyed and judgmental voice of my Garmin GPS. But when I envisioned a new life where I no longer felt like everything I did was wrong, I felt hopeful. I dreamt about moving into a place that was mine and when I'd wake up, I was sad to have left its safety and tranquility.

It was now late 2015, and we were going to visit my dad in Nashville for Thanksgiving. This was the first big holiday at his new house, and all of my extended family would be there. One afternoon, my dad called and told me I could invite my mom if I wanted to. He said he had plenty of room, and it might be nice for the boys to spend the holiday with both grandparents.

Sidenote: I feel like I need to set the stage for how crazy this first sounded to me. Besides my graduation and wedding, my parents had not been in the same room since I was six years old. I had not spent a holiday with *both* of them in over thirty years. It took me a minute to answer.

"Um, yes, I'd love to invite her, but are you sure? It wouldn't be weird for you?" I asked.

"No, it's fine. She's welcome to come," he replied.

So, I extended the invitation, and surprisingly, my mom accepted. I didn't know what to expect. My mom and dad had started communicating more after having grandkids. When Jack was in the NICU, I know they prayed together on the phone. I'd like to think this was when the tide turned for them. It allowed them to put all their drama in the past and unite as a team for my boys and me.

Everything was off to a great start, and on Thanksgiving morning, we started the day with mimosas. My cousins and I were imbibing steadily, but unbeknownst to me at the time, one of them had just found out she was pregnant. So, she was only drinking the orange juice, while her sister and I were downing all the champagne. I wasn't keeping track of how many I'd had.

By early afternoon, I was drunk.

Drinking on an empty stomach for several hours had me feeling warm, fuzzy, and a bit nostalgic. I remember sitting on the porch with everyone, and then, suddenly, it was just me and my mom and my dad. Adam was inside with the boys watching a movie. Everyone else had dispersed around the house.

An emotion began to envelop me that I can describe only as a tidal wave. It started at my feet, small and manageable. But within minutes, it was up near my waist. My breathing sped up, and suddenly it was up over my chest. My heart began racing, and the feeling was up to my neck. I took a deep breath, and it hit its peak over my head.

For my parents, my tears started as if out of nowhere but for me, it was a powerful release that had been a long time coming. I didn't just start crying; I began sobbing. I'm talking shoulders-shaking, gasping-for-breath, full-on weeping.

And this all happened in a matter of seconds. I'm assuming my mom and dad looked at each other with concerned expressions, but I couldn't see through the blur of my tears.

"Chandra, what's wrong?!" my mom implored.

The words were out of my mouth before I even had a chance to organize them.

"I don't want to be married anymore," I wailed.

Between heaves, I finally glanced up at my parents' concerned faces. I saw empathy and compassion in both sets of eyes.

A few seconds later, my dad said, "Then we'll figure it out. It's all going to be okay."

With those words, calmness washed over me momentarily, and it was during this pause that I looked up into the window of the kitchen—the window behind which the rest of my family was now standing. This included Adam and my two children, who were now crying hysterically. They'd been watching their mother fall apart, and rightfully so; it scared them.

Adam opened the porch door and stuck his head out to ask if everything was okay. His tone seemed both concerned and annoyed. In a quick moment of emotional control, I confirmed that, yes, everything was fine. I lied and said I had become overwhelmed talking about Beth's death. I explained (and this part was true) that being with both of my parents during a holiday for the first time in decades had affected me more than I had anticipated. And, of course, the two bottles of champagne didn't help.

I wish I could say I cleaned myself up and joined my family for Thanksgiving dinner. But the truth is, I missed the meal and went upstairs to lay down. Various family members came to check on me, but I didn't want to talk to anyone. Adam was confused and angry, but I didn't care. The only thing I could do was hide in my sanctuary under the covers. I squeezed my eyes shut and finally passed out into a dreamless sleep.

The next day, Adam was understandably irritated with me. So, I sucked it up, put on my game face, and spent the day acting like nothing had happened. Neither of my parents mentioned what I'd admitted the previous day. I knew the conversation wasn't over, but now was not the time to dive into these choppy waters. We finished our visit without any further theatrics and, a few days later, headed home.

Like most of our problems, Adam and I swept the incident under the rug. However, he occasionally brought it up in front of friends—the story of how his wife got wasted on Thanksgiving and had a meltdown in front of her family. Part of me thought he didn't actually want to know why I was crying that day. Maybe he even correctly assumed it had something to do with him. At any rate, I would laugh good-naturedly when he shared the tale, knowing deep down it was only a matter of time before the words "I don't want to be married anymore" came forth from my lips once again.

FUMES

After Thanksgiving, it became obvious our marriage was running on fumes. We spent Christmas with Adam's parents and argued the whole time. Then, we had a massive blowout on New Year's Eve. We could barely stand to be in the same room most days.

It had become clear we brought out the worst in each other. It's like we triggered the other's sensitive spots, poking at nerve endings just to get a reaction. It reminded me of how it felt to be constantly aware of someone else's mood, always walking on eggshells, just like thirty years before.

Around this time, my dad offered me his first relationship advice, and I still think about it to this day.

"A relationship is like a tree," he said. "And hurtful words and actions are like an axe. A tree can handle a few hits of the axe. But after enough strikes, the tree will inevitably fall over. A tree cannot withstand an infinite number of blows."

I knew our tree was toppling, but I couldn't yell "timber" to warn the innocent bystanders. The words "I don't want to be married anymore" lived at the tip of my tongue. They just sat there, not yet ready to come out, but no longer able to go back into hiding.

It's like they were frozen under some kind of spell—just waiting for the event that would bring them to life and unleash them into the world. I didn't know what would end up breaking the curse, but my inner knowing told me it was coming.

I would repeat the words "I don't want to be married anymore" in my head, over and over. I would do this in the shower, when I was driving, taking out the trash, and doing the dishes. It was as if I was daring them to come out.

And then one day, they did.

On a Sunday morning in late spring, we had taken the boys to breakfast. I was enjoying the comforting smells of coffee and maple syrup. A John Mayer song played in the background, and I was humming along. Then, while I was perusing the menu, I felt something small and wet hit my face. James and Adam both erupted in laughter as I saw what the errant object was.

A spitball. My husband had shot a spitball at my face and was now laughing about it with my son.

It was as if life suddenly shifted into slow motion. I sat and stared at him for what seemed like hours, but was probably only seconds, before jumping up and running to the bathroom. I sat on the toilet seat and cried. I cried out of embarrassment and shame. I cried because my husband thought so little of me that firing a wad of paper covered in his saliva seemed like a good idea. And I cried because he was teaching my five-year-old son to laugh at this act of disrespect.

By the time I came out, eyes red and puffy, the food was already on the table. I received a half-ass apology and let it go. I pushed it down with all the other emotional bullets fired at me over the years. But the bullet reservoir must have reached its limit. That space in my heart couldn't hold one more.

The thing you need to know about me is when I'm done with something, I'm *done*. I will give you a million and one chances to right wrongs and mend bridges. I will forgive and (try to) forget over and over and over. But when a behavior still doesn't change after all those chances? When the final proverbial straw has cascaded to the ground, I am done for good.

As we drove home from running errands later that morning, the words living at the edge of my breath for so long finally came out.

"I don't want to be married anymore," I stated matter-of-factly.

"What?" he responded. "Oh my God, if this is because of the spitball thing, you're totally overreacting."

"No. It's not just because of the spitball thing. It's because of all of the hundreds of blows to our tree. It's fallen over, and there's no saving it. I don't want to be married anymore."

Silence.

It's possible he was trying to figure out what I meant. It's also possible he knew exactly what I meant. We didn't speak for the rest of the drive. We didn't speak when we got home. He left on a work trip the following morning, and we didn't speak for three days.

I spent that time reviewing the past seven years of our marriage. A knot in my stomach wouldn't allow me to eat, and tears continuously fell after the boys went to bed, soaking my pillowcase each night. I weighed the pros and cons of staying versus leaving to ensure I was making the best decision. Not just for me, but for my kids, too. I could not watch my sons grow up and treat me with such blatant disrespect. I could not let them grow up thinking this is what a happy marriage looks like. I wanted more for them. I wanted more for myself.

When he got home, four days after I'd dropped the bomb, he said, "I guess we should put the house on the market."

So that's what we did. We made a plan to sell our house. His parents were getting ready to sell theirs as well and offered to let him rent from them temporarily. I finally started looking at apartments and found the perfect space for me and my boys. I even messaged my high school friend to let her know how her post had inspired me and that I was starting down my new path as well.

Adam never really tried to talk me out of it. I kept waiting for some kind of grand gesture. Not necessarily a holding-a-boombox-outside-the-window type of gesture, but flowers, a love letter, something. Looking back, I think he thought I was bluffing. I don't think he realized his last chance had come and gone. The final straw had shot a spitball at me, and I could no longer pretend.

We didn't speak much about the impending divorce, but as we packed up our things, half went into one trailer (mine) and half into another (his). The kids were so young and didn't really understand what was going on. My apartment wouldn't be available until October, so in August 2016, I moved into Adam's house until my place would be ready. This eased the transition for the boys, and we had another couple of months together as a family.

This was the *in-between*, when I spoke about teetering on a precipice. Even though I had made up my mind to leave, I was sad. I was sad to be breaking up my family. I was sad to know I wouldn't see my boys every day. I was sad this life we had been creating together for nine years was ending.

I remember one specific day in late August. I had been feeling incredibly anxious. Those same intense panicky emotions from my cutting days had returned. I paced the living room but couldn't think past the palpable fear in my chest. I called Adam and asked him to come home early from work. He walked in to find me bawling on the couch.

"What if I'm making a mistake?" I cried. "What if I'm making a terrible mistake?"

He sat down and calmly said, "Now this is the Chandra I know. You're finally making sense."

Amid panic and fear and hysteria was the Chandra he "knew." The Chandra questioning her own decision-making capabilities was "finally making sense."

I realized in that moment there were two Chandras. There was the version I *had* been. The one who made herself small to ensure everyone else was happy. The one who kept her shame and guilt shoved down with snark and wine. The one who had endured a relationship that made her feel lesser than. *That* was the Chandra he "knew."

But I was no longer that Chandra. The Chandra emerging like a butterfly from her chrysalis was different. I dried my tears and steadied my resolve. Although I still didn't know who this new version was, I knew I was no longer the person I had been.

My new wings were sprouting and would carry me onto my new path. The journey back to myself was just beginning.

PART THREE:

THE UNLEARNING

"The only thing that was ever wrong with me was my belief that there was something wrong with me. I quit spending my life trying to control myself and began to trust myself. We only control what we don't trust. We can either control ourselves or love ourselves, but we can't do both. Love is the opposite of control. Love demands trust. I love myself now. Self-love means that I have a relationship with myself built on trust and loyalty. I trust myself to have my own back, so my allegiance is to the voice within. I'll abandon everyone else's expectations of me before I'll abandon myself. I'll disappoint everyone else before I'll disappoint myself. I'll forsake all others before I'll forsake myself. Me and myself: We are till death do us part. What the world needs is more women who have quit fearing themselves and started trusting themselves. What the world needs is masses of women who are entirely out of control."

—GLENNON DOYLE

CHAPTER 8

Sometimes the lessons from the learning phase of our lives *do* serve us and can help us become better versions of ourselves. Experiences from which we learn how to feel empathy for another human being, for example. Or the times we learn to listen to our inner voice.

But other times, we realize certain beliefs no longer ring true. We have evolved, changed, grown. This is when it's time to unlearn the things that have been keeping us small. A time to unlearn the coping mechanisms that perhaps worked at one time but are now holding us back from becoming the people we're meant to be. A time to unlearn the roles we've played for so long and figure out who we really are.

To find my way back to me, I had to unlearn long-held beliefs. I had to question my deep-seated unworthiness. I had to figure out how to use my new wings.

***

BEGINNINGS

In October, I moved out of Adam's house and into my apartment with all my belongings and an array of emotions: excitement, sadness, fear, confusion, hope. At any given moment, I was simultaneously elated and devastated. While hanging my old clothes in my new closet, I alternated between tears and laughter. The dream I'd had of my own place with the boys had come true. I was on the alternate path. It was all happening.

James and Jack helped me set up their room with matching superhero bedding and hordes of stuffed animals. I decorated the rest of the house in a similarly cozy fashion. I wanted it to be a soft place for us to land, literally and figuratively.

Adam and I had agreed on splitting everything equally in the divorce, including our time with the boys. We decided on a week-on/week-off custody cadence, allowing Adam to travel for work. The first few nights in the apartment, the boys were with me. Then, on Halloween, the plan was for Adam to come over and we'd take the kids trick-or-treating in my new neighborhood. Afterward, he'd take them back to his house, and I'd have my first kid-free week.

My little Captain America and Teenage Mutant Ninja Turtle joyfully filled their plastic pumpkins with candy. When we got back to my place, it was time to say goodbye. Brave face on, I hugged and kissed them both, told them I loved them, and I'd see them soon. The door closed behind them, leaving a deafening silence.

A cold sweat crept across my forehead. My hands began to shake.

I sank to the floor and sobbed, knowing I wouldn't see my kids for a week. I crawled up the stairs to their room and lay down in Jack's twin-sized bed. I snuggled James' favorite blanket (aptly named Blankey) and breathed in their smell.

I probably cried for an hour, my tears soaking Iron Man's face on the pillowcase. It was such a release to let it all out. I think I had been holding in more than I even realized.

I would repeat this meltdown many times during that first year. Each new milestone would shake loose a fresh torrent of tears. The first time I wasn't there for a lost tooth. The first time I couldn't comfort them when they were sick.

The first holidays spent apart. That first Christmas I wasn't with them; I couldn't get out of bed all day.

Now that I've been doing this co-parenting thing for five years, I have the gift of perspective. I've seen the light at the end of the tunnel, but at the time, it was debilitating. I wavered between Superwoman—when the boys were with me—to a disaster when they weren't. I was terrified they'd feel even the slightest sense of the abandonment I'd felt as a kid. I was so afraid I'd miss out on important moments. And the truth is, I probably did. But I've also been much more present when I *do* have them. Those moments together are much more treasured.

As Adam and I began this chapter of our relationship as exes and co-parents, we entered uncharted territory. I knew he had started dating other people, and I too felt ready to meet someone new. I joined an online dating app and started swiping. In my journal, I'd requested a slightly nerdy gentleman who wore glasses and had a daughter. Someone who was empathetic and had high emotional intelligence. Someone passionate about live music like I was.

Just weeks after I moved into my new place, I found him.

My online dating profile picture was of me lying on the Hollywood Walk of Fame next to Lionel Richie's star. I'd always been fascinated with the singer and thought the photo was cute and a little quirky, like me.

I sent Nick a smiley face emoji, and he replied with, "Hello, is it me you're looking for?"

I was hooked.

We met on a Sunday afternoon. It was the first time I'd been out with someone new in nine years. I had to poll my girlfriends on what people even wore on dates anymore. I felt like an imposter in my ruffly top and high heels, all the while wishing yoga pants and flip-flops were acceptable first date attire.

As I drove to the restaurant, my nerves got the better of me. Anxiety rushed in, causing my mind to race and my stomach to plummet. By the time I parked, I was contemplating turning around and heading home. But I steadied myself and walked through the glass front door.

I saw him sitting at a table, looking just as nervous as I felt, which calmed me down.

"Hey Nick, I'm Chandra!" I said as he looked up and smiled.

"Hey Chandra, it's so great to finally meet you!" he replied.

His hazel eyes turned down slightly at the edges and made me think of a puppy. His black-rimmed glasses and plaid shirt gave off a hipster vibe. I just remember thinking he looked so kind.

He stood up, and we hugged each other. Then we sat on our respective sides of the table and began what would become one of my favorite dates ever. It was a night that would alter the course of my life, and the beginning of a relationship that would eventually bring out the best (and worst) in me.

ENDINGS

Nick and I talked for hours about life, parenting, marriage, and music. We had so much in common and felt like we'd known each other for years. When the date was over, we both stood up and began walking toward the door.

The restaurant was crowded, and in some moment of unguardedness, I grabbed his hand. It felt natural, and he squeezed mine back. We held hands all the way to my car and hugged goodbye. When he leaned in closer, I didn't have to think. To this day, it was one of the most perfect kisses I've ever experienced; the spark between us undeniable.

After our first date, we became inseparable. Whenever my boys were with Adam, and Nick's kids (a son and a *daughter*!) were with their mom, we spent time together. We saw concerts in Boston and Portland, visited breweries all over New Hampshire, and even flew to see my family in Nashville. We would spend slow, quiet mornings together drinking coffee and listening to music. We laughed all the time. I remember putting together a kitchen table one Sunday afternoon. We laughed about nothing and everything for hours. It was perfect.

I had fallen hard and finally felt like I'd found my person. *This* is what had been missing before. This mutual respect, love, and fun were what my soul had craved. I was happier than I'd ever been in a relationship, and was ready to go all in.

Adam and I had created a rule: Before a significant other could meet our boys, we had to date said person for at least six months. Also, the other parent had to meet the new love interest. So, after six months, Nick, Adam, and I sat down for an incredibly awkward exchange.

Nick and I sat on one side of the booth, and Adam flopped down across from us.

I made some small talk, commented on the traffic, but the tension was thickening. My old love and my new love, sizing each other up across the sticky table.

"Adam, this is an opportunity to ask any questions you might have before Nick meets the boys," I began.

Adam dove right in. "Well, I just want to make it clear that I'm their father. I want to make sure you know you're not to reprimand them in any way, and I don't think it's a good idea for you two to be physical in front of them. No hand-holding or kissing. This is all new, and we need to do what's best for them."

Nick responded calmly, "Yes, I respect all of that. I would never assume a father role with your kids, and Chandra and I will introduce each other as friends initially."

"Sounds good. Look, I'm late to be somewhere. I'll talk to you guys later," said Adam and just like that, he was gone.

Looking back, I know Adam was hurting. I know it was incredibly painful for him to see me in love with someone else so soon after our split. I felt and still feel compassion for him in that situation. I tried not to wave my relationship in his face, but it was impossible to ignore how happy I was. I knew he'd been dating other women and I hoped he'd meet someone just as perfect for him as Nick was for me.

Nick and I met each other's kids at a birthday party in late May. It went well, and we made plans to do more things with both sets of kids. It felt like we were moving toward merging our little families and starting a new one together.

And then things began to change.

I could sense him pulling away, and he started making excuses for why we couldn't spend as much time together. When we went to visit my mom in Florida in late June, he was just different. He stopped looking at me the way he had in the beginning. The laughing became more infrequent, and I'd catch him staring off into space. It was like he had checked out of the relationship.

One night after we got back from Florida, I brought it up. Through liquid courage, I told him I could feel him pulling away from me. I was still so in love with this man and saw a future with him. He admitted he was feeling overwhelmed and worried everything was happening too quickly. He thought we needed some time apart to figure out what we both wanted.

Knowing what I know now and having healed much of my abandonment trauma, his reaction was completely normal and one I wish I had met with compassion and faith. Instead, I felt a wave of slow, intense anger begin to build up inside of me. With alcohol fueling the fire of my rage, tears and biting words spilled from me.

"Why are you doing this to us?" I wailed. "I gave you everything! I introduced you to my family, to my kids, and this is how you treat me? This isn't how it's supposed to end!"

The difference between an argument with Nick and an argument with Adam was simple: Adam fought back. That's the response I was used to getting. It's what I was looking for—some kind of reaction. But like a turtle retreating into its shell, Nick shut down.

I didn't know what to do with the silence, so I pushed on. I yelled louder. I cried harder. All my unresolved abandonment trauma reared its ugly head, and feelings of worthlessness and shame overtook me. I assumed that him breaking up with me meant I wasn't worth loving. I didn't deserve my happy ending. These last eight months meant nothing, and I was destined to be alone forever.

These feelings of inadequacy led me to text him constantly, asking him to change his mind. I cringe as I write these words. It's no wonder he continued to retreat. I knew at the time this behavior was immature and unhealthy, but this experience was actually a turning point for me. Something was changing because I didn't do the one thing I had done since the crickets. I didn't play the one ace I always had up my sleeve when life got hard.

I didn't hide.

I put my feelings on the line and got rejected, but this time, I didn't seek sanctuary in anything external. I didn't turn to drugs or cutting or sex. I sat in my pain, and I felt it. I let its heaviness seep through my body, slowing now and again, but never staying put. It moved through me and, finally, I was able to release it.

The idea I had carried with me for decades—that if things get hard or messy or scary, it's okay to hide—had never served me. So, in the process of recovering from this painful experience, I unlearned it. I unlearned that hiding keeps me safe. I unlearned that staying small and quiet keeps the pain away. Those beliefs had served me at one point in my life, but no more.

I was done hiding. I would no longer stay small and quiet. I was ready to meet the person I'd been chasing all these years: ME.

FIRES

It took a long time for me to heal from my breakup with Nick and move forward. In fact, we got back together several times over the following four years. I dated other people but continued to hold out hope that someday we'd end up together.

In the meantime, Adam began dating a woman we both knew when we were married. Emma was someone who had helped out with the boys when they were younger. She herself was ten years Adam's junior but mature for her age.

She and I went shopping once and were asked if we were related. Both blonde and blue-eyed, she has eight inches of height on me and legs that seem as long as my whole person. She is beautiful inside and out.

Shockingly, my initial reaction to this news was indifference. Adam told me one afternoon on the phone and I believe my exact response was, "Okay. Thanks for letting me know."

This may seem like an unusual response to finding out your ex-husband is dating someone you know, but part of me was relieved he'd met someone. I could release some of the guilt I'd been carrying about moving on. Or maybe I was just in shock.

Whatever the reason, the longer I sat with the information of them dating, the more my attitude changed. Little things became big things. I knew the six-month rule didn't apply to her since she already knew our boys. I was aware of how much Adam's parents liked her while their feelings toward me had diminished since the divorce. The unfairness of it all started in my chest, a spark on a pile of kindling.

Less than an hour after I hung up the phone, smoke from the forest fire in my chest had risen to my eyes. Angry tears streamed down my face, and indignation seized my body.

What on earth was he thinking?

Why couldn't he have moved on with someone I didn't already know?

Why did he have to become such a cliché?

Adam and I fought about his new relationship often in the first few months of their dating. I worried it would be confusing for the boys. It was confusing for me.

I'm not proud of the things I said and the way I treated Emma in the beginning. For months, I wouldn't be in the same room as her. I didn't want her at the boys' birthday parties. I didn't want her picking them up from school. It felt too much like an attack on my status as their mother.

But, like every lesson I've learned and unlearned, I needed to hurt in order to heal.

It started slowly, but I began to acknowledge her presence. I invited her to James' birthday party at a trampoline park.

I complimented the cake she made him. My heart stopped throbbing when I saw her with Adam. We had become cordial.

Then one day in the car, James confessed, "I have some news, but Dad told me it was a secret. I really want to tell you though."

Intuitively I knew. Adam and Emma were on vacation in Greece, and I knew.

"You don't have to tell me, buddy, but I think I might know what it is," I replied. "Is Dad going to ask Emma to marry him on their trip?"

"Yes!" he replied enthusiastically.

"How do you feel about that?" I asked.

"I'm excited for her to be our stepmom!" he responded and smiled out the window.

The look on his face was not one of confusion or sadness. He looked happy. And isn't that all I want for my kids? To feel happy and safe and loved?

Something began to shift in me that day.

Upon their return, I drove over to the house they shared and congratulated her in person. I hugged her and welcomed her to the family. The weirdest part is, I meant it.

Adam and Emma announced their engagement in the spring, and by the fall, they announced her pregnancy. The following March they got married and a month later, their son, Jayden, was born on Jack's sixth birthday.

Our new modern family was beginning to take shape.

CHAPTER 9

Healing work is just that...it's work. It takes grit and determination to uncover the truth. It also requires compassion and empathy to navigate what's found. Healing asks you to stare directly into the face of the fire-breathing dragon and tame it through love and kindness.

Healing work can test your faith and help it grow. It makes you go back in order to go forward but can push you past boundaries you didn't realize existed. It can lead you down new roads you never imagined for yourself.

Such a road began to appear for me, and the course of my life changed once again.

***

TRUTHS

I firmly believe life doesn't happen *to* us; it happens *for* us.

Everything I went through with my dad gave me a perspective I may not have otherwise. If I hadn't experienced the struggles, maybe I wouldn't appreciate the relationship we have now.

I was meant to marry Adam so we could have James and Jack. Our hard times taught me about boundaries—what I was willing to put up with and what I wasn't.

I was supposed to meet Nick to feel unabashed love. To let down my guard and be vulnerable again with a man. Our relationship reminded me of what was possible. It also helped me look more objectively at my other relationships.

All the emotions I'd felt around Adam and Emma's relationship helped me find clarity on what's really important. They took a magnifying glass to parts of me I still needed to heal.

It was through the process of recognizing these lessons that forgiveness became an option.

When I was in my twenties, I went to Los Angeles with a friend. We stayed in the pool house at her aunt and uncle's house. One night after dinner, I was complaining to my friend about my dad. I went on and on, lamenting about how he'd never been there for me as a child and rarely as an adult.

My friend's aunt overheard me talking and, without preamble, simply stated, "Chandra, you can be a victim your whole life or, one day, you can forgive him so you can move on."

I was shocked and more than a little bit annoyed. Who was this woman to say such a thing to me?

A freaking truth-teller is what she was.

Her words sat with me for years. The more I thought about them, the more I realized she was right. I knew, even back then, the first step in my healing journey would be to forgive my father. Not for him, but for me.

Forgiveness is a tricky thing. It isn't about letting someone off the hook or saying what they did was okay. It isn't for *them* at all. Instead, forgiveness is a gift that allows *you* to drop the heavy burden of resentment so you can finally be free.

I knew I wanted to forgive these men in my life who had hurt me in different ways. But more importantly, I wanted to forgive myself.

To do so, I needed to heal my original abandonment trauma, or my fears around being left and unwanted were going to suffocate any future relationships. I started reading books, listening to podcasts, and joining online webinars about personal development. I began practicing something I'd learned about.

Something called inner child healing.

Inner child healing "is a way to address our needs that haven't been met as children and heal the attachment wounds we've developed...By healing our inner child, we begin to create the safety and security our younger selves have always needed. By doing so, the positive traits of our inner child have room to shine. We unlock our natural gifts, our inner curiosity, and our limitless capacity to love." (*Mind Body Green*, 2020)

In other words, it's a way to give love and compassion to the unhealed parts of yourself.

This can be done in a number of ways. I've listened to meditations, spoken with life coaches, and read as much as I could find on the subject. Through all this immersion, I developed my own practice. I'm not exaggerating when I say learning how to heal past traumas and reconnect with my younger self changed my life.

It may sound simple, but the first step in my inner child healing practice is to have what I call a wallow day. I try to limit it to a day, but if it needs to be a little longer, that's okay too. We grant ourselves limitless grace when we're in the process of healing.

During my wallow day, I allow myself to just feel my feelings. I let myself feel frustrated, angry, sad, or any other emotion that comes up. The goal is to *feel* the feelings, but not get stuck in them.

If I need to cry, I cry. If I need to scream, I scream. If I need to journal it out, I journal it out. If I need to watch something sappy or a movie from my childhood, then I do it and I don't judge myself. I let myself wallow for the day and feel all the things because I know I will approach the next day very differently.

Usually by the second day, I've released most, if not all, of the negative emotions just by validating and experiencing them fully. The next step in the process is to become the observer of the feelings. I put on my detective hat and get to work. I ask myself probing questions, such as:

What were the specific emotions I was feeling?
What triggered those emotions?
Can I remember a time I felt this way before?

Maybe I'm not able to go back to the very first memory of experiencing that emotion, but I try to go back as far as possible. Most times, it's a memory from childhood.

I try to bring forth the memory and observe it from my mind's eye, almost as if I'm watching it on a movie screen. I watch my past experience, and when the scene has reached its peak of intensity, I enter as my adult self and go to sit next to my child self.

As though I was comforting one of my own children, I ask her what she needs. If she wants to be held, I hold her. If she wants to talk, I listen. If she has questions, I try to answer them as best I can with my adult self's wisdom and knowledge. I tell her whatever I intuit she needs to hear. I let her know she is loved and worthy and perfect. I let her know things will get better and everything is going to be okay.

Then I come back into the present moment and write down everything I told my little self. I journal out the entire experience with as much detail as I can remember. Usually, by this point, I'm emotionally exhausted and need to take a break, so I put down what I wrote and go do something else for a bit. Then later, I read through the words my adult self shared with my child self.

As I read them, I imagine the words are coming from a trusted source to my current adult self. And nine times out of ten, it's exactly what I need to hear at that moment. Whatever lesson I was looking to glean from my wallow day can be found in those words. They are a message directly from my inner knowing—my authentic self.

This process proves to me that everything we need to grow and evolve is already inside of us. Therefore, there is no need to look externally, only within.

In her book *What Happened to You*, co-written with Dr. Bruce D. Perry, Oprah Winfrey notes, "Your past is not an excuse. But it is an explanation—offering insight into the questions so many of us ask ourselves: Why do I behave the way I behave? Why do I feel the way I do? For me, there is no doubt that our strengths, vulnerabilities, and unique responses are an expression of what happened to us." (Perry and Winfrey, 2021)

"Very often," Winfrey continued, what happened "takes years to reveal itself. It takes courage to confront our actions, peel back the layers of trauma in our lives, and expose the raw truth of our past. But this is where healing begins."

Peeling back the layers of trauma in our lives. Shining a light on them and getting curious. This is how we forgive. This is how we heal.

MEETINGS

By 2019, I was perched high atop the corporate ladder. I had managed the US communications team for a global chocolate company for five years and was great at my job. I created meaningful connections with influencers. I grew brands through visual storytelling on social media. I built strong relationships with co-workers, many of whom are still close friends. Hell, I even got to go to the Golden Globes and the Emmys.

But as healing work will do, it forced me to be honest with myself. Not just in my personal life, but now also in my career.

Similar to my marriage, I'm sure my job looked "perfect" on Facebook, but behind the scenes, I was ferociously treading water and gasping for air. Commuting over two hours a day to sit in meetings for nine hours was slowly consuming my soul. I had no freedom, always beholden to someone else's timetable and needs. I wasn't allowed to make any decisions without running them by several other people, most of whom didn't actually understand what I did or had some other agenda.

I felt trapped. The golden handcuffs of a six-figure salary and celebrity hobnobbing kept me silent.

I remember one specific meeting after a high-visibility public relations event. I had worked on the idea for over nine months, and not unlike giving birth after the same gestation period, I thought of the project as my baby. The positive media coverage poured in, and I was so proud of my team for making the experience successful.

As I shared the results with our global leadership team, I was confident I'd finally be able to excite this group of older European men who were not easily impressed. Celebrities had shared photos of our event on their social feeds. *US Weekly* wrote an entire feature about it. The media impressions were already hitting tens of millions, and as I finished my presentation, I paused, waiting for the inevitable round of applause.

But it never came. Instead, I was chastised about the quality of the celebrity photos and repeatedly questioned over the accuracy of the numbers. Suddenly, it felt like I was on the witness stand and pleading for leniency against false accusations. The event I'd worked so hard on for nearly a year was deemed "meh" by a room full of men who could never, and would never, understand the value I brought to the table.

I strode into the room a confident lioness. I slinked out of the room a skittish kitten.

That particular meeting was a breaking point for me. For months afterward, I constantly felt stressed and on edge. I began to question every move I made. I never felt good enough, and yet, I felt like I owed it to the company to stay.

Every morning, my alarm would blare at 6 a.m., daring me to start another day. I'd hit snooze for an hour, all the while staring at the ceiling, willing myself to check my phone. The familiar pit in my stomach would return as I looked at all the unread emails, the meetings on my calendar, and my never-ending to-do list.

Resentfully, I'd throw off the covers and get up. I'd make it through the day with a plastered-on smile, knowing I wasn't making a difference and didn't have a voice. Exhausted and burned out by the evening, I'd crawl into bed only to rinse and repeat the following day.

The stress at work undermined much of the healing work I was doing in my personal life. I knew it wasn't sustainable, but I was still too afraid to admit what I really wanted: to be my own boss.

Sure, I had daydreamed about working for myself someday, but had never legitimately considered myself an entrepreneur until I began to heal my past trauma. Through that process, my confidence was growing, and my sense of self was getting stronger.

Suddenly, the idea of managing my schedule, working when and where I wanted, and not having to take part in corporate politics anymore became intoxicating. I began to envision myself working from coffee shops, writing copy while I sipped on cappuccinos. I got excited at the prospect of setting my own hours, no longer commuting every day, and not worrying about how many hours of face time I put in at the office. The thought of no more meetings made my heart sing.

I had worked in marketing and communications for over fifteen years at that point. I knew what I was doing, and I had contacts. Every time I thought about going out on my own, it felt like my future. It felt like the right decision.

Healing helped me realize I no longer wanted to climb the corporate ladder. I wanted to build my own.

SIGNS

Before I could quit the cubicle life altogether, I still had more inner work to do. My spiritual awakening began with Gabby and grapes.

If you're wondering why each new journey of mine starts with a book, it's because they have the power to change perspectives and open up worlds. *The Universe Has Your Back* by Gabby Bernstein was no exception. (Bernstein, 2016)

I had never been super religious. When I was little, I went to the Methodist church with my grandparents in the summer and on weekends with my dad, but I spent most of the time drawing on the back of the offering envelopes. I joined a "mega" church in my twenties, but in all honesty, I was there for the free coffee, live music, and socializing. When I got married, I converted to Catholicism so we could baptize our babies, but I haven't been to a service since my confirmation. Again, not what you would traditionally call religious.

I have always felt like there was something bigger than me, but I wasn't sold on all the rules and guilt associated with some organized religions. I am as liberal as they come, so a house of God that doesn't welcome everyone makes no sense to me.

The God I pray to is love, plain and simple. I have never felt like I needed to sit in an uncomfortable pew to worship. I talk to God every day. On my couch. In my bed. I refer to God by lots of names. Universe. Infinite Intelligence. Source. The Big Guy (or Gal) Upstairs. The God I believe in doesn't care which name I use.

When I picked up Bernstein's book, I was curious to understand more about her perspective on God and spirituality in general. I was beginning to admit to myself I wanted to leave my corporate career, but I was scared of the unknown.

I was listening to the audio version one evening on my way to meet a friend for dinner. The chapter playing through my car speakers was one in which Bernstein explained how to ask for a sign from the Universe.

"Asking for a sign means that you're willing to collaborate with the Universe. It means that you're committed to releasing structure and control to instead be led by a power greater than yourself," Bernstein shared.

"Remember and trust that the Universe has a better plan than you do. You can ask for a sign to guide you toward anything you desire. If you're unsure about a decision or you simply want to know you're on the right track, ask for a sign. And don't get hung up about what your sign should be. Just choose the first thing that comes to your mind. Just let whatever comes to your mind become your sign. Allow it to come to you naturally and commit to what you hear." (Bernstein, 2016)

It wasn't the fact that she looked for signs that blew me away, but how *easy* it was to ask for one. So, on my drive to dinner, I spoke aloud.

"Okay, Universe, Gabby said this would work and that I should trust the first thing that comes into my head. So, what's my sign?"

The reply came to me clearly.

Grapes.

The word "grapes" appeared clear as day in my mind. I could see it written out in front of me in big, bold letters.

"Grapes? Really?" I laughed. "That's my sign?" Nothing. Silence. So, I begrudgingly moved on and waited for my grapes. I do like wine, I thought. Maybe that's the connection.

I pushed it from my mind and met my friend for dinner. About five minutes into our conversation, she says the word "grapes." I can't remember the context, but my eyes widened, and she looked at me funny. I told her what had happened on the drive over, and we both got chills. From that moment on, grapes became my sign.

I started to see them everywhere. In movies and TV shows (side note, the TV show *New Girl* mentions grapes in no fewer than three separate episodes). In my kids' homework and books ("G" is for grapes!). God bless the popularity of charcuterie boards because they appeared daily in my social media feeds.

Every time I saw or heard the word "grapes," I'd smile. A warm, comforting feeling washed over me, and I knew the sign was meant for me. To let me know I was on the right path. To tell me I wasn't alone.

Grapes even led me to my first retreat.

One day I was scrolling through social media and saw a photo of grapes in a random post. I smiled and felt drawn to continue down the page.

Just underneath, I saw an advertisement for a yoga retreat at a Buddhist monastery in the Santa Cruz mountains. I can't explain the pull except that it just felt *right*, like it was the exact kind of experience I needed to continue down my spiritual path. So, I signed up, booked a flight to San Francisco, rented a car, and drove the seventy-ish miles to Soquel, California.

As soon as I entered the gates, I knew I was in the right place. Prayer wheels and Buddha statues greeted me. There was a quiet I'd never known before, a peace I felt immediately.

For three days, a group of twelve women ate together, practiced yoga together, hiked together, and relaxed together. Each of us from different parts of the country, we bonded over delicious vegetarian cuisine prepared by the monks themselves. Awestruck, we gazed at redwoods in the forest and enjoyed spa treatments from traditional Chinese healers.

One such healer paused in the middle of my massage to ask me about the tattoo on my left shoulder. She recognized the Chinese symbol for "snake," the Chinese year in which I was born.

"Those born in the year of the snake are intuitive, but can be quiet," she said. "You are a good person, but you do not yet recognize your worth. This tattoo is a good reminder for you. You know what the snake can turn into?"

"No," I whispered quietly.

"When she knows her power, the snake can turn into a dragon," my healer replied. "The dragon is a symbol of strength and good luck. Know your power and you too can have strength and good luck."

Since those early days of my spiritual journey, I've asked for additional signs and noticed other synchronicities. The latter come mainly in the form of angel numbers. Angel numbers are number sequences you see everywhere. On clocks. On license plates. On receipts. For me, I see 444 at least once a day.

According to one article I read about angel numbers, "If you're navigating a challenge, and have been trying to get guidance from your spirit guide or signs from the Universe, noticing the number four all around you can serve as evidence that you're being heard." (*Well and Good*, 2021)

So, whenever I check my watch and it's 4:44, I smile and send a little prayer of gratitude upwards. I know that this number, grapes, and all my other signs are all breadcrumbs from the Universe. Gifts to help direct me down my path, confirming I'm living in my truth and getting closer to my authentic self.

Grapes were an integral step on the journey back to me. These little winks from God built my faith that everything would work out. My inner knowing was once again guiding me toward my truth, and I was listening.

AWAKENINGS

Once I embarked on my spiritual journey, I began to see life and humanity differently.

According to author and spiritual leader, Deepak Chopra, "One of the first signs of awakening is *noticing*. You may be going through life on autopilot without giving much thought to who you are, what you want, and why you are here. Having these questions pop up is like turning on a light in a previously dark room." (Chopra.com, 2020)

Oh, I was noticing, alright. I was beginning to ask existential questions. I wanted to understand why I was here, what my purpose in this life was, and how I could find more fulfillment.

And the answers were coming to me. Anytime I got still and thoughtful, I would have these aha moments. They often became clear through journaling, during the quiet hours of my commute, or just before falling asleep at night.

Little messages would appear in my mind's eye. I would jot down whatever wisdom came to me in the notes section of my phone. The consistent theme that kept pushing through? We are all here for a reason. We all have a purpose. Each of us has access to the answers if we trust ourselves enough to listen to our inner knowing.

The twist is, not only do we all have a purpose, but I think we all have the same purpose. I believe our purpose in this life is to realign with our authentic selves. Let me explain.

I believe we're all born as our true selves, and then the world begins to condition us. Society, family, teachers, and communities shape us with their rules and expectations. Boundaries are placed on us, and we conform to the identities that make everyone else feel safe. This is the learning phase we covered in the first part of this book.

As early as childhood, we're assigned roles. Implicit biases from the grown-ups in our lives label us. The smart kid. The cute kid. The funny kid. The good kid. The bad kid.

In high school and college, we take on new roles. If you've seen *The Breakfast Club*, you know all about the athlete, the brain, the princess, the basket case, and the criminal.

Even as adults, we're cast into roles. The parent. The spouse. The employee. Judgments are assigned. Good or bad. Successful or unsuccessful. Right or wrong.

The world becomes starkly black and white.

The truth is, none of these roles actually define us. Not our true selves. They're just the parts we're assigned to play. The costumes designed to hide who we really are. It's up to us to decide whether we keep playing along or tear them off and allow the world to see us, the real us.

Perfectly imperfect. Scarred in the most magnificent ways. Walking miracles.

I hid behind these roles for so much of my life. All the phases I went through in high school and college were just a dress rehearsal for the main event—taking on the roles of wife and mother. These were society's crowning jewels.

Every societal expectation was like a domino on my life's path. Each one was carefully placed and protected to keep harmony with the status quo. That is, until my midlife renaissance, the re-awakening that allowed me to see past the roles and begin the journey back to myself.

In the words of renowned psychiatrist Carl Jung, "Your vision will become clear only when you can look into your own heart…Who looks outside, dreams; who looks inside, awakes." (Brainy Quote, 2021)

Over the years, I've worked to find the real me, the true me. While it took several years, lots of tears, and so many books, we've finally been reacquainted. And she's everything I ever wanted.

She's everything I'd been searching for all those years. She's the voice I've always heard in my mind and in my heart. She's the sense of safety I've never been able to feel with someone else. She feels like home.

She's always been there, just beneath the surface, waiting for me to leap so she could become my wings.

CHAPTER 10

If you've ever visited an optometrist for glasses or contacts, you know what it's like to peer through the phoropter machine (yes, I had to Google what the instrument is called). Your chin rests on cold plastic as you try to make out the letters on the opposite wall through two thick lenses. The doctor will then adjust some dials and, suddenly, you can see. Everything becomes clear.

The Universe had become my optometrist, and the way I viewed the world shifted. I was able to see things through a new lens.

Working in a corporate environment no longer felt safe for me. Like those too-tight jeans I wore for so long in my marriage, I knew the time had come to take them off.

When I stepped off that cliff of my marriage in August 2016, my wings formed. I began to relish the unknown and grow in ways I never would have expected. And now, four years later, I was ready to see if they'd keep me in flight as I made the second giant leap of my life.

***

RETREATS

I cleared the path to leave my job for nearly a year. I brainstormed my company name and created my LLC. I made business cards and started an Instagram account. I added to my savings account and paid off debts. I even landed my first official consulting client while I was still in corporate.

But I still hadn't put in my notice, too afraid of the *what ifs*. *What if I fail and have to crawl back to a corporate job? What if other people think I'm making a huge mistake? What if they're right?*

Then I picked up a book called *Don't Keep Your Day Job* by Cathy Heller.

"When you hear that inner wisdom whisper, 'You are here to do something great,' listen up! You are about to be led to the exact opportunities that will empower you to share your unique talents with the world." (Heller, 2019)

It's like she was conspiring with my inner voice to wake me up. *You left a marriage, Chandra! You can most certainly leave a job.*

I devoured the book and then sent her a message on Instagram sharing how much it had moved me. To my surprise and delight, she responded. In fact, she shared an invite to a special retreat she was hosting at her home a few months later.

I felt the same pull I had previously followed to the yoga retreat at the Buddhist monastery, and I knew I had to go. Retreats quickly became my transformative vehicle of choice as so much change could take place in such a condensed amount of time.

In a moment of déjà vu, I signed up, booked a ticket to California (this time Los Angeles), and took an Uber to the cutest Airbnb in West Hollywood.

The next morning, I arrived at Cathy's home early. I got my coffee and journal ready and found a seat in the cozy circle of chairs and pillows. Once all ten women were seated, Cathy began.

She told us candidly about her tumultuous childhood. She explained how she never felt like she was enough, even well into adulthood. She shared her own version of inner child healing with the group and six-year-old Chandra squealed with delight.

We took some time to journal on specific prompts and then share our musings with a partner.

What were you like as a child?

What messages did you receive as a child from your parents?

Can you remember a time in childhood when you felt unworthy of love?

Cathy then walked us through a meditation where we comforted our younger selves. I had never experienced inner child healing in a group setting, but it was powerful. The vulnerability these women shared after only knowing each other for a few hours was inspiring.

By the afternoon, we were all talking about our passions. The hopes, dreams, and fears that, for some, had never been uttered aloud. Each of us pouring out words of encouragement and support for the other women who had been strangers just hours earlier.

And then Cathy had us do an exercise I still remember vividly to this day.

"Everybody, sit up straight and close your eyes," she began.

"Imagine you're inside a house looking out the window. One person shows up on the lawn and stands there smiling. Then another joins, and another. Within seconds, the front yard is blanketed with smiling individuals. Within minutes, the street and entire neighborhood."

Cathy continued, "What if each one of those smiling people was someone you helped by following your passion and by going after your dreams? What if by doing what lights *you* up, you were able to light *them* up? Standing in front of your house are the millions of people you've touched and impacted. And the millions of people they've touched and impacted because of you. All of them, sending you love and gratitude. Can you feel it?"

In my mind I saw them. Millions of women I had inspired or empowered in some way. I didn't yet know how I would do it, but I felt the promise of it happening. *There is a bigger reason I'm here*, I thought.

Tears streamed silently down my cheeks and splashed onto the pages of my journal, smearing the ink of my truth. Joy swirled through my chest. My heart tingled.

"Now, imagine what happens if you stay where you are and don't follow your passion, don't go after your dreams. What does your life look like in five years? In ten? In twenty? How do you feel?" Cathy went on.

An ache replaced the tingling. I pictured myself still in my cubicle. Years of disappointments having taken their toll; I was a shell of who I used to be. The woman sitting there was bitter and anxious. She was afraid of making decisions and had lost the spark that used to draw others toward her.

Cathy finished up the visualization exercise with the following: "Lastly, think of those millions of people from before who were standing in front of your house. Millions of people you could have impacted, but didn't, because you were afraid. And be honest with yourself. Which scenario is worse? Being scared to take the leap and follow your dreams? Or knowing that you could have had the life of your dreams and didn't because you were too afraid?"

I flew back to New Hampshire the following day knowing what I needed to do.

ZONES

Before my divorce, back when I was checking all of society's boxes and hiding behind my various roles, I was not pushing boundaries. I was living for other people and playing small. I had hunkered down right in the center of my comfort zone.

One *Forbes* article defines the comfort zone as "the state of mind in which a person feels totally at ease and away from possible danger or mistakes. While this sounds like a good thing, it can be dangerous if you want to do and continue doing something extraordinary." (*Forbes*, 2021)

My definition? The comfort zone is a behavioral construct that minimizes risk and maximizes the status quo. It is a "place" that exists to keep us safe from the unknown. It is the headquarters for our ego.

Our ego is the part of our identity that thinks it has all the answers and is allowed to judge right and wrong. For the ego, things are simply black and white. The late spiritual leader, Wayne Dyer, defined ego as "Edging God Out." (Dyer, 2010)

He continued, "Ego, the false idea of believing that you are what you have or what you do, is a backward way of assessing and living life."

I think what Dyer meant is, when we live in our comfort zone, we associate our worthiness with external things. Our bank account, our career title, our dress size. So, in my mind, that would mean the only way to reclaim our self-worth is to step *outside* the comfort zone. *Away* from the ego.

People tend to stay in their comfort zones, not because they are comfortable—as the name would have you think—but because leaving them is scary. When you're outside the perimeter, everything is different and new. For good reason, I've seen the zone just outside the comfort zone referred to as the fear zone (*Positive Psychology*, 2020).

Any slow meandering out past the confines of your personal comfort zone can come to a screeching halt when suddenly met with the "monsters" of disappointment and the unknown.

These monsters don't exist in the comfort zone because the comfort zone doesn't allow for risk. There is no chance for disappointment. And because the comfort zone is all about control, there is no room for the unknown.

For so many, staying in the comfort zone becomes a lifelong goal. In contrast, others know everything they've ever wanted lies just outside those walls. And those curious adventurers who pack up and leave to explore the great unknown? Those people make magic.

According to an article in *Psychology Today*, "Whatever your comfort zone consists of, you pay a huge price for it. Life provides incredible possibilities, but you can't take advantage of them without facing pain. If you can't tolerate pain, you can't be fully alive. There are many examples of this. If you're shy and avoid people, you lose the vitality that comes with a sense of community. If you're creative but can't tolerate criticism, you'll never reach people who could appreciate (and fund) your work. If you're a leader and can't confront or set limits with people, no one will follow you. By staying in the comfort zone, you end up relinquishing your most cherished dreams and aspirations." (*Psychology Today*, 2012)

I found myself on my own adventure after leaving the comfort zone of my marriage. Of my Facebook-perfect life. Of the status quo. And I met those monsters. Yes, I experienced many disappointments on my journey and trepidation as I faced the unknown, but it was worth the risk.

Unlearning my ego and leaving my comfort zone were not easy tasks. My spiritual awakening pushed me through the barrier, leaving me alone and unprepared on the other side. As I entered the fear zone, wide-eyed from wariness and excitement, I repeated the Glennon Doyle mantra and name of her podcast: *We Can Do Hard Things*.

I soldiered on, and only when I was outside the walls of my comfort zone did I see how small it was—tiny even, compared to the vast expanse of potential that lay before me.

Only then, while I was facing my fears head-on, did I realize that just beyond the fear zone lies the learning zone. The learning zone is where you acquire new skills and deal with challenges. All you learn (and unlearn) in this zone helps you evolve and move forward into the final frontier: the growth zone. This is where your aspirations are realized, and where you get to live your dreams (*Positive Psychology*, 2020).

The growth zone is a place of fulfillment and alignment with who you are. On Maslow's hierarchy of needs, this is self-actualization. The pinnacle of realizing your potential. The limitless zone where you can reconnect with your authentic self. Because again, I believe *that* is our purpose—going home within ourselves to find peace.

Once I answered the call of my inner voice, there was no going back. I knew I was meant for more. I craved freedom and flexibility. I needed space to honor the ebbs and flows of my energy. I deserved to feel inspired.

My healing journey and spiritual awakening transformed me. I was finally ready to leave the comfort zone of my career.

PIVOTS

On January 31, 2020, I packed up my desk and walked out of the office for the last time.

The first six weeks were everything I'd envisioned. Networking opened doors for new clients. Inspiration poured through me. I even worked from coffee shops in Nashville for a week, writing copy and sipping cappuccinos just like I'd imagined.

And then, in mid-March 2020, a global pandemic rocked the entire world.

I flew back from Nashville just as the panic set in. On my way home from the airport, I stopped at a CVS for toilet paper. Unfortunately, there were just two rolls left—and not the good kind.

Along with everyone else, I was now terrified of so many things that only days before had been normal. Going to the grocery store now warranted a hazmat suit (or at least a homemade mask made from a bandana and hair ties). In-person school was canceled and transitioned to "remote learning." My kids were now home all day and, apart from the daily sixty-minute Zoom calls with their actual teacher, the responsibility of their education fell on me.

Wine sales went up, and the question of whether Carole Baskin killed her husband was all anyone could talk about (answer: of course, she did). Not to mention there was a *deadly virus* floating around out there that any of us could catch just by breathing.

If starting a business is hard, then starting a business at the onslaught of a global pandemic is excruciating.

The networking halted. The inspiration dried up. The coffee shops closed.

I needed some help and support on what was quickly becoming a very lonely journey. I needed a mentor, someone to learn from who was further down the entrepreneurial road than me. I reached into my savings and hired a business/life coach.

She helped me in more ways than I could have imagined. Yes, she provided me with some tactical tools to grow an online business. But more importantly, she became the next step on my healing and spiritual journey. Through my coach, I learned how looking inward could help me be more productive. I started a morning routine of mindfulness and meditation. I continued to journal, made a vision board, and read books about manifestation and the law of attraction.

Realizations began bubbling to the surface. I wanted to help those feeling like I had before the leaps away from my marriage and career—stuck, lost, trapped. What if I was here to inspire and empower other women to find their greater purpose by reconnecting with their authentic selves?

All of this deep introspection made something clear to me: I wanted to be a coach myself.

Similar to when I recognized I no longer wanted to be married or climb the corporate ladder, admitting this shift to myself felt right. It felt like the next breadcrumb on my path.

Of course, all the old demons of comparisonitis and imposter syndrome rose to the surface. Once again, I questioned my own worth.

Who am I to do this?
Why would anyone listen to me?
What are my qualifications?

Life/career/business coaching was still a relatively new concept and, as such, fairly unregulated. Also, I'm not a licensed therapist, so I wasn't exactly sure how I could help others. But something my coach told me rang true, and I clung to it as I embarked on this new adventure.

"There are always going to be people in front of you and people behind you on life's path. You can learn from those ahead of you and guide those behind you. Your ideal coaching client is someone who is ten feet behind you. She can't yet see twenty, thirty, forty feet ahead of her, only ten. Therefore, you can be the beacon of light and guide her along those ten feet," she shared.

So that is what I did. I listened, supported, and guided women as they leapt from their comfort zones. I relayed the stories of what I went through and how I came out on the other side. I shared everything I had learned on my healing and spiritual journeys with women just starting on their own.

Eventually, I pursued certifications in career coaching and life coaching, but honestly, these were more for my own sense of accomplishment. Most of what I needed to know could be found in those early words of my coach.

The truth is, we are drawn to people for a reason. I was drawn to my coach because she was the one who was meant to help *me* move forward ten feet. And my clients were drawn to me for the same reason.

As Elizabeth Gilbert writes in her book, *Big Magic*, "The Universe buries strange jewels deep within us all, and then stands back to see if we can find them." (Gilbert, 2015)

I held the mirror so they could see their own greatness. And in doing so, I recognized my own.

LESSONS

Being an entrepreneur was confusing at times. My practical side felt like it was constantly battling the spiritual, the right brain arguing with the left. Masculine energy versus feminine energy—always tension back and forth. But in that push/pull scenario, I also found a balance that was new for me.

I wanted to meditate, journal, and drink tea all day long, but I also wanted to promote my business and book new clients. I thought I had to do one or the other, but it turns out, doing *both* is what helped me on my path to purpose.

That combination of hustle and flow has allowed me to feel alignment *and* support myself financially. When I start to lean one way too heavily, I consciously do something to shift. If I'm too in the hustle and feeling anxious or stressed, I schedule a few hours of rest. I go for a walk, get a massage, or sometimes, just take a nap. And when I'm too languid and start feeling lazy, I schedule a few hours of work. I sit at my desk and hunker down with my to-do list.

That lesson was one of many I learned in my first year of entrepreneurship.

Another was that, in order to survive, I needed to unlearn a lifetime of people-pleasing behaviors. I needed to remember to prioritize inner over external validation. I've since realized other people's opinions of us are actually none of our business. The only thing we have control over is our reaction to what we experience.

I was so afraid to leave my career for fear that other people would think I made a huge mistake. And many did. All I had allowed them to see on social media was the highlight reel, so of course they felt that way. Even well-meaning family members asked the anticipated *"Are you sure?"* and *"What if it doesn't work out?"* questions. But, if I had let their fear make my decisions for me, I would not be where I am today.

We get to choose whether to believe something. We get to choose what move to make next. Our inner peace is what matters, not what someone else thinks or says. I've realized the only person worth comparing myself to is a previous version of me. Growing and evolving are the only true measures of success.

Another lesson I picked up that first year was that there will always be great days and shitty days. The trick is to keep going. Remember, we can't have light without dark. As with everything in life and nature, ebbs and flows are inevitable.

Somewhere along my entrepreneurial journey, I signed up to join a program with a male business coach.

He promised us we'd be making five-figures a month right away and went so far as to give us a script for discovery calls. A discovery call in coaching is when you chat with a potential client about where they are currently, where they want to go, and what's standing in their way.

"Follow my script, and you'll book clients left and right," he'd said.

I'd had some success on previous discovery calls, but I wanted a consistent queue of interested coaching clients. On my next discovery call, I decided I'd use his script. About fifteen minutes into the call, the woman on the other end of the line stopped me and said she was feeling really uncomfortable. The questions I was asking were too aggressive and she didn't think we'd be a good fit.

I hung up the phone feeling defeated and frustrated. Why didn't it work? I quoted the script line for line! I repeated his words just the way I was supposed to.

His words. Not mine.

Maybe that script worked for him, but I am not him. If I'd trusted my inner knowing and used my softer approach, I likely would have had the honor to coach her. Instead, I followed my fear-based ego and rushed into a conversation that neither of us were ready for.

That failed discovery call was actually a wake-up call.

Once we begin to view failure as inevitable, it becomes less scary. Failure can act as feedback on how to do something differently the next time. When we learn to embrace the bad days as learning opportunities and lessons, we alchemize their power to heal.

A final lesson I'll share, and the one I've found to be the most important and enjoyable, is to follow what lights you up. Do the things that feel good in your soul and bring you pure joy. Because in doing those things, new opportunities begin to appear seemingly out of nowhere.

I worked with one client who, at forty-two years old, felt lost and stuck, but knew she was meant for more. During our work together, she realized that instead of being a home improvement influencer (which is what she had been doing), she wanted to pursue two things: 1) to write and 2) to be more involved in her community.

Once she acknowledged all her badassery and got clear on what she wanted, she put her trust in the Universe that things would work out. She began saying "yes" to things that lit her up and "no" to what didn't.

An hour of yoga this morning? Yes!

A brand partnership that doesn't feel aligned? No!

That's when the Universe showed up for her in a big way. She was standing in her driveway one afternoon, and a neighbor pulled up. He told her he thought she would be perfect for a particular role he was looking to fill—a digital content creator for a local magazine.

She had never mentioned her newly discovered desires to him. She just made clear to the Universe what she wanted, trusted the process, and followed the opportunities that brought her joy. She has now been in that role for nearly a year and loves it.

After our time together ended, she sent me the following note: "Chandra, you helped me find clarity in my path and my purpose, and together we excavated my values and strengths, some of which I didn't realize I had. I now feel so much clearer and more confident in the direction of my life. You taught me how to use my inner compass and trust it to show me the way. Thanks for helping me grow into who I'm meant to be!"

I instantly remembered Cathy's exercise and imagined this amazing woman as the first one standing in my yard. I began to cry tears of gratitude.

Realizing I had that kind of impact is humbling. It made me even more grateful for having gone through everything I did, accumulating the lessons, and using them to help others.

In addition to universal life and business lessons, launching a business during a pandemic taught me more about *myself* than I ever would have imagined.

I realized how brave I was. I tried new things and took risks. Without knowing where it would lead, I followed that inner knowing and never doubted it would put the right people, ideas, and opportunities in my path.

I realized how resilient I was. I was told "no" so many times, and it just made each "yes" that much sweeter. I fell down over and over but kept getting back up.

I realized how much I needed freedom. Having been in corporate roles for nearly twenty years, I had become accustomed to rules and limits. I thought they were real and solid, but they were illusions. They were only sleights of hand conducted by those at the top, trying to keep everyone productive and in line.

Without all the healing work I did, without my spiritual awakening, and without my entrepreneurial journey, I would not be the woman I am today.

CHAPTER 11

The woman I'm becoming isn't perfect. I still have days when I want to hide. Days I feel unworthy of love and simple kindnesses. Days when it all feels like too much.

But then I look back at all I've been through. With time, it has become clear that obstacles doubled as teachers. Each lesson learned and unlearned brought me to the person I am today. I am more me than I've ever been, and I've finally embraced all my quirks and imperfections.

I've worked so hard to clear the debris from my path and will continue to do so for the rest of my days. On this journey of life, the finish line is not important. It is the small moments each day when I make a conscious choice to love and accept myself that matter. When I'm able to love and accept others just as they are, I feel myself expand. When I realize none of us have the answers, I allow myself to relax.

For me, this is peace.

For me, this is growth.

For me, this is everything.

***

HIKES

Once Emma became a mother herself, our relationship blossomed. We understood each other on a new level, now as teammates in the rough and sometimes painful contact sport of motherhood. We began communicating more frequently, offering support where we could, celebrating the big and small wins of each of our boys.

When Jayden was about six months old, we took all three boys on a hike. With the baby strapped into his carrier, the five of us made our way up a family-friendly path in the White Mountains of New Hampshire.

First, we chatted about James and Jack. How big they were getting. How they were adapting to the new school year. How sensitive and sassy they both were. How exhausting and exciting they made our lives.

At the top of the peak, we stopped and ate turkey sandwiches on a large gray rock. I asked a traditional family to take a photo of our modern one. With full bellies and huge grins, we posed for the first shot of the five of us.

Before heading home, we stopped at a local brewery for a cold beer after a long day. Adam joined us before taking all three boys back to his house so Emma and I could have another drink together.

This was the first chance she and I really had to sit down just the two of us. We both saw this as an opportunity to wipe the slate clean, to begin anew. So, we talked...for over two hours.

One beer turned into several. We talked about the past few years. About her feelings and my feelings. About this new family we were creating.

I apologized for how I'd treated her when I found out they were dating. She apologized for putting me in such an awkward position. We recounted old memories we shared and talked about our dreams for the future. We cried and hugged. Finally, Adam had to come pick us up because we were both a little drunk. I consider that day a new beginning for us.

Since then, we text nearly every day. Sometimes it's about the kids. Sometimes it's a funny TikTok video. Adam, Emma, and I are on a group text where we discuss all things co-parenting. She is always a part of the conversation.

My current relationship with Adam is a little more layered. I've told people that sometimes I feel like he's my brother. I care about him and want good things for him, but I can only be around him for short periods of time before I want to punch him. I'm kidding. Mostly.

The truth is that we don't always agree on things, but we love our kids and do our best to get along for them. And really, it's a win-win for everyone involved when we're able to put our past differences behind us and work together for the sake of our family. Because as unconventional as it may seem, we *are* a family.

We depend on each other. Emma and I don't have any blood relations nearby, so this little crew is all we have. For us—maybe more than Adam—this family has become our stability, our sense of home.

Thank God we had that support because soon, Jack would face his second near-death experience at only seven years old.

ACCIDENTS

I was on my way to have dinner with a friend when my phone rang, and Adam's name flashed on the screen. It was his week with the boys, and they were on a camping trip. Adam and Emma frequently took the boys on such trips in their RV, but this was a new campground all the way in Pennsylvania, about ten hours away.

"Hey, what's up?" I answered.

In a calm voice, Adam responded, "Jack has been in a bike accident. We're on our way to the hospital."

"Oh my God!" I cried. "Is he okay? What happened?"

"He was riding his bike too fast down a hill, and his brakes weren't working. He took a sharp turn and crashed into a parked golf cart. He was wearing a helmet but has a concussion and a gash in his leg. I'll call you back when I have more information."

I was scared, but Adam's steady demeanor comforted me. I figured if Jack was seriously injured, Adam wouldn't be so composed.

I was wrong.

I was only five minutes from the restaurant, so I decided to continue to meet my friend. I explained to her what had happened and I may need to leave early. She completely understood and an hour later, my phone rang again.

This time, Adam's voice was wavering. "Jack has a fractured skull. They're running a bunch of tests to see if there's any bleeding in his brain. They don't know how severe it is yet, or if there will be any permanent damage. I'll call you back when I know more."

I burst into tears and ran to my car. I called my mom and began hyperventilating.

I wondered if I should I drive straight there. It was now close to 7 p.m., so if I left now, I'd get there by five or six in the morning. Mom talked me out of that plan, as it wasn't safe for me to drive in my distraught condition.

Instead, she and other family members began looking for flights as I shakily drove the ten miles back to my house. My friend followed behind just to make sure I got home safe. In fact, she sat in my house with me and said she wouldn't leave until I had a plan (sidenote: Get yourself a friend like this).

I couldn't focus. All I could picture was my baby lying in a hospital bed, wanting his mama who wasn't there. The guilt was gnawing on my heart. Finally, I found a flight that would get me into Harrisburg, PA by 11 a.m. I would be with my baby before noon the following day.

I called my best friend to see if I could stay over. She lived near the airport and was home on maternity leave with a newborn, so I knew she'd be up a lot that night. She said of course, so I threw a bunch of random clothes into a suitcase and drove to her house. We sat and talked until close to 3 a.m. before we finally tried to get some rest. I fell in and out of sleep until 6 a.m. and then drove to the airport.

Adam hadn't given or been given many updates. Jack was conscious, and there didn't appear to be fluid in his brain, which was great news. They finally flushed and stitched up his leg, but he was in pain.

I had FaceTimed with ten-year-old James for a few minutes the night before, and the terror in his voice was raw.

"Jack is the glue that holds this family together," he cried. "I can't imagine life without him."

Through tears of my own, I did my best to let him know things would be okay, even though I knew I couldn't promise anything.

I thought of this conversation as I sat at the airport gate. I pulled out my journal and furiously wrote a message to Jack.

You're in the hospital in Pennsylvania right now, and I'm beside myself. I cannot lose you. You are my bright shining star, and the world needs you in it. I love you so, so much and am sending all my love to you right now. Mama is so scared. I'm getting on a plane to come see you. Everybody is praying for you. You have to be okay. I can't wait to see you and give you so many kisses. Stay strong, my little one, and you'll come out on the other side. I've sent all my guardian angels to watch over you. You are one of my favorite people in the world. I'll see you soon, my love.

I spent the rest of my trip praying the way I had learned when Jack was born—covering him in love and golden light. It was the only thing I knew to do.

By the time I got to the hospital, Jack was already sitting up and eating. He was tired but talking. Adam and I were able to give him a shower and wash off some of the previous day.

The doctor came in and told us how lucky Jack had been. If he hadn't been wearing his helmet, he would likely have brain damage, or worse.

For the second time in his life, Jack defied all odds, and as he tends to do in these life-or-death situations (aka his birth story), he made a complete recovery within twenty-four hours. He was discharged with stitches, antibiotics, and instructions to lay low for two months.

On the drive back from the hospital, Jack said, "I guess God kept me here because I'm meant to do more things in this world."

I believe this with all my being and cannot wait to see all the amazing things this little guy will do.

FEATHERS

Since they were camping in rural Pennsylvania and there weren't many lodging options, Adam invited me to stay in the camper with them until my return flight three days later.

This was gracious—and awkward. I enjoy spending time with Adam and Emma, but we weren't used to being together in such close quarters for an extended time. We had also just been through the traumatic experience of almost losing Jack, so we were in a bit of a haze and emotions were running high.

Being so up close and personal with Adam's new life affected me differently than I expected. I wasn't jealous per se, as I know very well we are not meant to be together. But there was some element of me feeling lonely, and not a little like a third wheel. I felt uncomfortable and confused, unable to make sense of my uneasy gut.

After one sleepless night, I got up early and went for a walk. I decided to traverse the route Jack had been on when he had his accident.

As I retraced his path, I noticed two seemingly random things that stuck out in my mind.

The first was the name of the road. In the weeks before I got married, my grandmother had been moved into hospice and I knew she wouldn't be able to attend the wedding. She was so distraught (we both were) so I promised to visit her afterward and show her the photos and videos.

When she passed away only days before the big event, our family (myself included) truly believed Grandma made the executive decision to move on early to get a front-row seat.

On my wedding day, as I began the procession outdoors, a chipmunk crossed right in front of me and sat on the side of the brick path. It stared at me the entire time, turning its furry little head as I walked down the aisle, following my every move. Something deep inside of me knew it was a sign from my grandmother. Just like the grapes, every time I see a chipmunk, I send up a little prayer of gratitude that she and my other angels are always watching over me.

The road Jack crashed on was called Chipmunk Road. I know in my heart she protected him that day.

The second thing that stood out to me on my morning walk at the campground was the beautiful gray feather I noticed lying in the road. I remember thinking I should look up what it meant and then, moments later, saw another one. I took out my phone and Googled the meaning. I stumbled upon an article about the spiritual significance of gray feathers.

"As a symbol across many cultures, feathers have always represented a connection to spiritual realms and to divinity. And because of their connection to birds, they have always been a symbol of flight and freedom, not just physically, but also in a mental or spiritual sense. Like a bird that soars through the boundless sky and has a view of all things from high above, feathers symbolize the ability to transcend and move beyond your mental barriers and limitations—to see the larger picture and understand what really matters." (WootAndHammy.com, 2018)

Something about that last sentence hit me. My emotions were raw, my stomach tied up like a ball of yarn. Perhaps these feathers lying in my path were a sign to zoom out at the bigger picture of life. I continued to read.

A gray feather specifically represents neutrality—"it is a sign that the world is not black and white, that there are many viewpoints to consider. A gray feather may be a reminder to step back and think about a situation in your life that may not have a clear answer. It asks you to read between the lines and to look for subtleties that may reveal another point of view or another way to think about or resolve a situation." (WootAndHammy.com, 2018)

Again, this felt meaningful.

If everything leading up to my midlife renaissance was a line of dominos, all stark black and whites, then what was this message trying to tell me?

What if I was supposed to look at the bigger picture and realize there was no *one* answer to anything. No absolutely right or absolutely wrong way to live this life. No 100 percent good or 100 percent bad people. No true black or true white.

Maybe it's all just shades of gray. Maybe *we're* all just shades of gray.

All my experiences have brought me to where I am today. Each time I didn't feel seen or heard. Each time I didn't trust myself. Each time I felt unworthy of love, respect, and support. Each of those experiences forced me to look deep within myself and provided an opportunity to heal.

As I continue down my path, I don't know where it will ultimately lead me. Like everyone else, I can only see the next ten feet ahead. But I will keep looking for signs and picking up breadcrumbs. I will keep shedding the roles that keep me small. I will keep unlearning the beliefs that hold me back from my authentic self.

For the rest of my life, I will keep finding my way back to me.

EPILOGUE

FALL 2021

The leaves are in their final act, showing off with their saturated spectacle of autumnal beauty. The reds, golds, and greens remind me of a Culture Club song and make me wish they'd stay this way forever. But the truth is, they're dying. This kaleidoscopic swan song is the last we'll see of these particular leaves before they fall to the ground and crunch beneath our feet.

One of my best friends hangs a banner in the fall that reads: *Autumn shows us how beautiful it can be to let go.*

Amen, sister. Letting go saved my life.

I'm currently in the White Mountains of New Hampshire, curled up in the window seat of my rented tiny house. My hair pulled up in a messy bun wearing glasses still smeared with the fingerprints of searching for them in the early morning dark. My second cup of coffee burns my tongue, and a crisp, cool breeze blows through the screens. Peace and contentment wash over me and an intense sense of gratitude inspires me to close my eyes and smile.

Here we are. We've made it.

Today, I no longer teeter on any precipice. I no longer wonder if I should honor my inner knowing. I no longer try to squeeze into too-tight jeans.

This book has healed parts of me I didn't realize were still wounded. The writing process unlocked memories and initiated difficult conversations. Not unlike birthing a baby, many parts were messy and painful, but what came forth was a tangible part of my inner self.

This book you hold in your hands is a piece of me.

A few weeks ago, I was in North Carolina at a writing retreat. Going into the three-day conference, I had only one expectation—to leave inspired. This seemed inevitable based on the theme of the weekend: Wild Awakenings. Instead, the awakening that took place was more subtle than wild.

We learned and wrote and shared during the day. But the true awakening occurred on the drives to and from the retreat center with my girlfriends. Singing at the top of our lungs to power ballads by Tori Amos and Ani DiFranco, laughing with each other while the wind tousled our hair, I realized something: *The more I love, the more I feel like me.*

When I am filled with love and gratitude, I am at my best. When I listen to my inner knowing, she leads me down the paths meant for me. I have so many plans for the future.

I will write more books. I still have so many stories to share and lessons to unlearn. Writing is how I express myself and typing the words I see behind my eyes brings me inexplicable joy. I choose to follow those things that light me up.

I will fall in love again. I know he's out there somewhere— an empathetic man who will show me a lifetime's worth of support and respect. A confident man who will make me laugh so hard I snort and will cry with me when we watch

This Is Us. A brave and kind man who is on his own healing journey and doing the work to become his best self.

I will open a retreat center to help others find their way back to themselves. A safe place for the weary woman still squeezing into those too-tight jeans. At last, she'll be able to rip them off without fear of being naked. Because we'll all be naked—no masks or costumes allowed. Only vulnerability and showing up as our most authentic selves.

Five years ago, I wouldn't have had these plans. Five years ago, I couldn't see what was possible. Maybe like the autumn leaves, parts of me had to die in order to be reborn.

Renewal. Reawakening. Renaissance.

I know now that life is not black and white, but all shades of gray. And maybe, just maybe, hidden within the gray are flecks of reds, golds, and greens.

ACKNOWLEDGMENTS

A special thank you to every single person mentioned in this book for being a part of my life and for teaching me something valuable.

To my boys, for being the brightest stars in my sky. You give me purpose and inspire me to become the best version of myself. I love you both more than you'll ever know.

To my mom, for always encouraging the girl who read the books to become the woman who wrote them. Mama, I will forever love you the mostest.

To my dad, for letting me share my stories. I know this process wasn't easy for you, but I am eternally grateful for your honesty and grace. I am so proud of this summit we've reached hand-in-hand, and the breathtaking views we get to witness together. I love you, Daddy.

To Maddie, for allowing me to share your story. You are one of the strongest and kindest women I've ever had the honor of knowing. I love you sissy—Team Alpha forever.

To Adam and Emma, for your support in writing this book. There's nobody else I'd want with me on this co-parenting adventure.

To my daily support system, I'm so lucky to call you incredible women my best friends:

To Cassie, for being my soul sister in this life and so many previous ones. There's no one else I'd rather be punny with.

To Marie, for being my rock (and travel buddy) throughout this journey. You are one of my favorite people in the world.

To Norie, for being my sister-cousin and supporting me at every turn. I was there when you were born, and you've been there for me every day since.

To everyone at the Creator Institute and New Degree Press, especially:

To Shana Heath, for making the writing process fun! You're such a light in this world.

To Julie Colvin, for pushing me to dig deeper and find my voice. I am so proud of what we've created.

To Eric Koester, for building this beautiful container of learning, support, and community.

To all my magical beta readers for your edits and encouragement: Marie Bucklin, Cassie Bustamante, Ann Czaja, Kristen Dallhoff, Kelly Forrister, Lindsay Fortin, Audrey Kennett, Tasha Lantz, Kelley Nayak, Laurie Paradis.

And finally, thank you to all of my early supporters who helped this book come to life: Michelle Arsenault, Jennifer Ash, Kristin Baker, Samantha Bartlett, Diane Bitsack, Leah Brown, Marie Bucklin, Amber Bui, Cassie Bustamante, Melanie Carson, Michelle Casserino, Chris Chittenden, Candace Cimon, Susan Costigan, Aislinn Creel, Maryam Cristillo, Ann Czaja, Kristen Dallhoff, Jennifer Davidson, Rebeka Davila, Sarah Michelle Davis, Sonja Dearden, Lindsay Delfa, Melisa Diaz, Kim DiCosmo, Jessica Dolan, Cindy Drislane, Kristina Drociak, Mairead Dunphy-Fabrycki, Jennifer Earhart, Leigh Enderle, Kirsten Engstrom, Amy Finnegan, Kelly Forrister,

Lindsay Fortin, Rachel Fox, Amanda Freudenthal, Nadja Fromm, Heather Garlich, Neha Goel, Carrie Halpern, Lindsay Hardie, Yeechin Harvey, Pam Hemenway, Krystal Hicks, Brandy Iturrino, Audrey Kennett, Earle Kennett, Janet Kennett, Peter Kessinger, Kishan Khona, Kim Kisil, Erin Klotz, Carrie Kocik, Eric Koester, Lauren Krasnodembski, Jaimi Lacaria White, Robin Lane, Erin Legare, Stephanie Lewis, Suad Mammadkhanli, Sarina McAllister, Elissa McGee, Bonnie Morata, Gina Nardi, Kelley Nayak, Dean Nguyen, Danielle O'Neil, Kelly O'Neil, Laurie Paradis, Kimberly Parets, Nicholle Perriello, Lexi Peto, Jillian Pierce, Colleen Plaut, Marisa Porter, James Rhodes, Sarah Riddell, Cady Roberts, Vivian Sawatzky, Toni Sayce, Cynthia Scala, Amy Schmid, Jennifer Schwalb, Melanie Schwartz, Jenn Seavey, Catherine Simms, Megan Skinner, Brittany Stageberg, Theodora Stanchie, Melissa Starin, Kate Sullivan, Alex Tacket, Meredith Thomas, Tanya Tobin, Julie Ulrich, Edwin George White, Courtney Whitmore, Norie Whittle, Emily Young, Amy Youssef, Aimee Zappa.

APPENDIX

AUTHOR'S NOTE
Melton, Glennon Doyle. *Love Warrior*. New York: Flatiron Books, 2016.

CHAPTER 1
Todd, Carolyn L. "14 Facts About Bipolar Disorder That Everyone Should Know." *Self*, September 27, 2018. https://www.self.com/story/bipolar-disorder-facts.

CHAPTER 2
Melton, Glennon Doyle. *Love Warrior*. New York: Flatiron Books, 2016.

Perry, Bruce D., MD, PhD, and Oprah Winfrey. *What Happened to You? Conversations on Trauma, Resilience, and Healing*. New York: Flatiron Books, 2021.

CHAPTER 3
American Psychological Association. "What is Cognitive Behavioral Therapy?" July 2017. https://www.apa.org/ptsd-guideline/patients-and-families/cognitive-behavioral.

RAINN. "Campus Sexual Violence: Statistics." Accessed August 5, 2021. https://www.rainn.org/statistics/campus-sexual-violence.

Rennison, Callie Marie, PhD. *Rape and Sexual Assault: Reporting to Police and Medical Attention, 1992–2000*. Washington DC: US Department of Justice, Office of

Justice Programs, Bureau of Justice Statistics, 2002. http://bjs.ojp.usdoj.gov/content/pub/pdf/rsarp00.pdf.

CHAPTER 4

Castillo, Michelle. "1 in 7 New Moms May Suffer from Postpartum Depression." *CBS News*, March 14, 2013. https://www.cbsnews.com/news/1-in-7-new-moms-may-suffer-from-postpartum-depression/.

Harris, Nicole. "What Is Chemical Pregnancy?" *Parents*, August 27, 2018. https://www.parents.com/pregnancy/complications/miscarriage/what-is-chemical-pregnancy/.

CHAPTER 6

Allard, Jody. "If You've Suffered from Vanishing Twin Syndrome, You're Not Alone." *Parents*, December 21, 2017. https://www.parents.com/pregnancy/complications/miscarriage/vanishing-twin-syndrome-is-more-common-than-you-thought/.

March of Dimes. "Placental Abruption." Complications. Accessed August 10, 2021. https://www.marchofdimes.org/complications/placental-abruption.aspx#.

CHAPTER 7

Brown, Brené. *Rising Strong*. New York: Penguin Random House, 2015.

Cutruzzula, Kara. "The Last 100 Years of Self-Help." *Time*, August 9, 2016. https://time.com/4443839/self-help-century/.

France, Kim, and Tally Abecassis. "All in for a Midlife Renaissance." December 8, 2020. In *Everything is Fine*. Podcast, 44:37. https://everythingisfinepodcast.com/index.php/2020/12/08/episode-37-all-in-for-a-midlife-renaissance/

Lexico (Powered by Oxford Dictionary). s.v. "renaissance (n)." Accessed August 20, 2021. https://www.lexico.com/definition/renaissance.

CHAPTER 9

Bernstein, Gabby. *The Universe Has Your Back*. Carlsbad, California: Hay House, Inc., 2016.

Brainy Quote. "Carl Jung Quotes." Accessed August 20, 2021. https://www.brainyquote.com/quotes/carl_jung_146686.

Estrada, Jessica. "What Angel Numbers Mean, and Why Seeing Them Everywhere Is Great News." *Well + Good*, May 28, 2021. https://www.wellandgood.com/what-are-angel-numbers/.

Lechner, Tamara. "10 Signs of Spiritual Enlightenment & Awakening." *Chopra*, September 21, 2020. https://chopra.com/articles/10-signs-of-spiritual-enlightenment-awakening.

Perry, Bruce D., MD, PhD, and Oprah Winfrey. *What Happened to You? Conversations on Trauma, Resilience, and Healing*. New York: Flatiron Books, 2021.

Trieu, Tiffany. "What is Inner Child Work? A Guide to Healing Your Inner Child." *MBG Mindfulness*, December 31, 2020. https://www.mindbodygreen.com/articles/inner-child-work.

CHAPTER 10

Dyer, Dr. Wayne. "The Ego Illusion." *Wayne's Blog* (blog). Accessed August 30, 2021. https://www.drwaynedyer.com/blog/the-ego-illusion/.

Gilbert, Elizabeth. *Big Magic: Create Living Beyond Fear*. New York: Riverhead Books, 2015.

Heller, Cathy. *Don't Keep Your Day Job: How to Turn Your Passion into Your Career*. New York: St. Martin's Press, 2019.

Heyward, Chastity. "Four Reasons Why You Shouldn't Remain in Your Comfort Zone." *Forbes*, March 30, 2021. https://www.forbes.com/sites/forbesbusinesscouncil/2021/03/30/four-reasons-why-you-shouldnt-remain-in-your-comfort-zone/.

Michels, Barry. "The Comfort Zone: Hiding in Plain Sight." *Psycholgy Today*, May 8, 2012. https://www.psychologytoday.com/us/blog/the-tools/201205/the-comfort-zone.

Page, Oliver, MD "How to Leave Your Comfort Zone and Enter Your 'Growth Zone'." *Positive Psychology*, August 25, 2021. https://positivepsychology.com/comfort-zone/.

CHAPTER 11

K, Norma. "What Does a Feather Symbolize?" *Woot and Hammy* (blog). January 2, 2018. Accessed August 30, 2021. https://wootandhammy.com/blogs/news/what-does-a-feather-symbolize-symbolism-signs.